Reading
Together

Reading
Together

· Share in the ·
WONDER of BOOKS
with a Parent - Child
BOOK CLUB

Written by Noah Brown, Dominic de Bettencourt, Ann Delehanty,
Kristin Doherty, Luci Doherty, Lissa Kaufman, Dana Lowe-Rogstad,
Owen Lowe-Rogstad, Michelle McCann, and Ronan McCann
Illustrations by Liz Kay

CHRONICLE BOOKS
SAN FRANCISCO

Library of Congress Cataloging-in-Publication Data available.

ISBN 978-1-7972-0515-1

Manufactured in China.

Design by Rachel Harrell.

Typesetting by Howie Severson.

10 9 8 7 6 5 4 3 2 1

Chronicle books and gifts are available at special quantity discounts to
corporations, professional associations, literacy programs, and other organizations.
For details and discount information, please contact our premiums department at
corporatesales@chroniclebooks.com or at 1-800-759-0190.

Chronicle Books LLC
680 Second Street
San Francisco, California 94107
www.chroniclebooks.com

TABLE OF CONTENTS

INTRODUCTION

Back in 2008, our group of five kids and five moms formed a neighborhood parent-kid book club. We parents did it because our kids were just starting to read on their own and we wanted to encourage their book-loving ways. They were also starting to build their first real friendships. We figured being in a book club together would give them extra time to play with their new friends. And a bonus—we could get to know some other parents better.

These were small goals. None of us expected the group to last more than a few years.

But our kids loved book club. Whenever we suggested scaling it back or quitting altogether (when they entered middle school and again at the start of high school), the kids refused. They even asked if we could meet more often, not less, and read more books! Those first graders are all grown up now. We've had one hundred book club meetings and have read one hundred books together. It still blows our minds.

Over the years, some members have left and new members have joined. The types of books we read together have changed. The depth of our discussions has changed. How we do our meetings has changed. But our love of reading has remained constant. And as our once-pint-size cutie-pies started to head off to college elsewhere, we decided to write this book together.

Over the years we've had lots of people ask, "How can we start our own book club?" And the follow-up questions: "How old should the kids be when we start?" "How do you find good books?" "What do we do at the meetings?" This book has answers to those questions and plenty more. It has everything you need to know to start your own group, run your meetings, choose great books, and adapt as your kids get older. With this book you can start a group just like ours, or bust out and do your own unique thing.

This book club has been a life-changing experience for us. We realize that it has been a tremendous privilege to be able to create a book club with our kids. We hope that this book describes a variety of ways that anyone can create a book club with the wonderful kids in their life, even if they face serious time crunches or other obstacles. Book club doesn't have to cost any money or take more than a couple of hours each month, and it can be a great way to spend some positive time with a child. We hope to inspire more kids to read books, more adults to read books, and more families to talk about books together.

So give it a try. You won't regret it!

ABOUT THE AUTHORS

Book club in first grade

Book club in twelfth grade

The Kids (from left to right)

Owen:

Most Likely To: Do a Drawing for Book Club

Most Like: Charlie from *The Perks of Being a Wallflower*

Favorite Books: *Where the Red Fern Grows, Ready Player One, The Absolutely True Diary of a Part-Time Indian, The Perks of Being a Wallflower*

Ronan:

Most Likely To: Pick *Another* Sci-Fi Book

Most Like: Gale from *The Hunger Games*

Favorite Books: *Daughter of Smoke & Bone,* the Harry Potter series, *Ender's Game, Ready Player One*

Dominic:

Most Likely To: Have an Obscure Trivia Question

Most Like: Greg from *Diary of a Wimpy Kid*

Favorite Books: The Harry Potter series, *Artemis Fowl, Ranger's Apprentice, The Hunger Games, Ender's Game, Diary of a Wimpy Kid, Insignia*

Noah:

Most Likely To: Pick a Rock Climbing Book

Most Like: Simon from *Lord of the Flies*

Favorite Books: *The Hate U Give, Touching the Void, The Absolutely True Diary of a Part-Time Indian, Dance of the Infidels: A Portrait of Bud Powell*

Luci:

Most Likely To: Pick a Book about Sports

Most Like: Katniss from *The Hunger Games*

Favorite Books: *The Hate U Give,* the Harry Potter series, *Every Day, Ready Player One, The Maze Runner*

The Parents

Dana (Owen's mom):

Most Likely To: Pick a Classic Book

Most Like: Laura from the Little House series

Book I Look Forward to Reading with My Adult Child: *A Prayer for Owen Meany*

Michelle (Ronan's mom):

Most Likely To: Have a Really Strong Opinion about a Book

Most Like: Meg from *A Wrinkle in Time*

Book I Look Forward to Reading with My Adult Child: *The Autobiography of Malcolm X*

Ann (Dominic's mom):

Most Likely To: Threaten to Pick *Little Women*

Most Like: Don Quixote

Books I Look Forward to Reading with My Adult Child: *Little Women, Don Quixote*

Lissa (Noah's mom):

Most Likely To: Pick an Adult Book

Most Like: Liesel Meminger from *The Book Thief*

Book I Look Forward to Reading with My Adult Child: *The Curious Incident of the Dog in the Night-Time*

Kristin (Luci's mom):

Most Likely To: Carry the Adults in Trivia

Most Like: Hazel from *The Fault in Our Stars*

Book I Look Forward to Reading with My Adult Child: *The Boy Who Runs*

A NOTE ON PROBLEMATIC AUTHORS

We recognize that some of the authors of our favorite books listed here (as well as authors included elsewhere in this book) have been or may be accused of racism, sexual harassment, homophobia, and more. We are not intending to ignore these issues or advocate that you support these authors and their books. Instead, we recommend that you do your own research about the books you choose for your book club to make sure those choices work for your group. See page 125 for more on this important issue.

Part 1

STARTING

YOUR
OOK CLUB

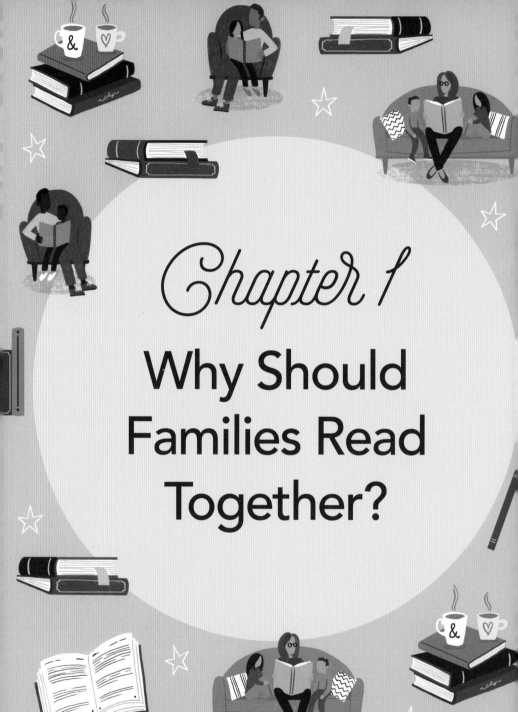

Chapter 1
Why Should Families Read Together?

"Nothing is hopeless;

we must hope

for everything."

—from *A Wrinkle in Time*
by Madeleine L'Engle

We know that a lot of people are busy, whether it's with work, volunteering, taking care of children, or running a household. Who has time to start a book club? But you also want your kids to read. In fact, you want them to *love* reading so that they don't stop when they get older and their phones, sports, and friends suck up all their time.

We're guessing that's why you're reading this book. Well, congratulations—you are a genius! Researchers have discovered that reading is good for kids. *Incredibly* good for them. In fact, it's one of the most important things we parents can encourage our kids to do.

Researchers at a number of universities around the world have found that a child's love of reading is one of the best predictors of future educational achievement, life success, and overall happiness. Kids in elementary school who read frequently for pleasure (five to seven days per week) are *way* more likely to go to college (regardless of socioeconomic background) and find more fulfilling careers. As improbable as it sounds,

reading will make your child's entire life better in lots of ways.

But how can you get your kids to read without nagging them? We can tell you from our experience, starting a parent-child book club is a fantastic way to get you *both* reading more. Being in a book club with you will help your child develop into a frequent reader and foster a lifelong love of books. And, best of all, you will have a great time doing it!

If you start a parent-child book club of your own, we believe:

Your kids will become (and stay) strong readers.

Ronan: I love reading, but English is *not* my favorite subject. I definitely prefer math and science, and most of my friends would never guess I'm in a book club. My favorite thing about the group is discussing books with my friends. It's always entertaining to hear what other people think about the books I like. Or don't like. And it's much more fun to talk about a book with other people rather than just reading it by myself. When I read a book by myself, I usually forget about it. Book club makes me *think* about what I read and hold on to it longer.

Dominic: Being in the book club has encouraged me to read more books. Not only read them, but go deeper into them. This is something I normally complain about doing for English class, but when it's with a book I like in book club, it's a lot more interesting. Then, when I have to do this kind of analysis in school, it's a lot easier.

Your kids will learn to push themselves, try new things, and think critically.

Noah: Being in the book club pushes me out of my comfort zone. I have autism and can be shy. Socializing during our meetings gets me to talk and helps me be more confident and successful in other social situations. My autism also means that when I am interested in a topic, I am *really* interested in it! I love being in the wilderness and I love jazz, so I gravitate toward nonfiction like *Into Thin Air* (about a Mount Everest climbing disaster) or *Dance of the Infidels* (about Bud Powell, a jazz musician from the 1940s). The other kids expect this by now. More often than not, they really like the books I choose. This pushes my friends out of *their* comfort zones and gets them to read books they wouldn't otherwise. It broadens all of our perspectives. I think it also helps them understand me better.

Owen: To be honest, when we started the group, I didn't care about the reading part. I was only interested in more time to play with my friends. I didn't realize then all the skills I would learn. Without realizing it, I gained so much knowledge about books, reading, critical thinking, and asking questions. These are skills I use every day in school, in all subject areas. While book club has definitely helped me in school, the impact has been much deeper. It's inspired a love of literature that has pushed my imagination and fueled my passions. Though I went to a math/science K-8 school and am good at those subjects, I recently discovered that I love storytelling and began writing in my free time. Now I'm going to study writing in college. Without the foundation book club laid down for me, I doubt I would have ever made that leap.

You will talk more easily with your kids about deep, meaningful issues.

Michelle *(Ronan's mom)*: Our book club has allowed me to be involved in so many deep conversations with my son, his friends, and my own friends about all the stuff we've read over the years. Being in a book club together gave me many opportunities to talk with these kids about their feelings on racism, sex, drug abuse, and many other complicated, important issues over the years. We've talked deeply about intimate stuff. For kids of any age to open up like that in front of a group is pretty amazing.

Dana *(Owen's mom)*: In the beginning, the highlights of our meetings were playtime and who won the trivia game. Over the years, the kids became much more engaged with the books. Some of the topics we covered provided a safe entry point into conversations with our teenagers about serious and important subjects. Even as they grew into young adults, the group helped us stay connected to our kids and to what was happening in their lives.

Luci: Being in the group has definitely helped me become a better reader and enjoy reading more, but what I love most is the people. These are friends I've known for more than ten years, and it's nice to get together every month and catch up. Over the years I have become much more appreciative of what book club has done for me. Not only have I been able to read and discuss so many great books, I've gotten to learn and grow with great people who I call my friends.

Ann *(Dominic's mom)*: Book club is great for parents too. Once we graduated from the "playdate" phase of parenting, it wasn't as easy for us parents to get together in a low-key way. Our group has been meeting throughout the ups and downs of elementary, middle, and high school. It's been wonderful to check in with other parents on how things are going and how their kids are handling each stage of this journey.

Your kids will develop closer friendships (and so will you).

Lissa *(Noah's mom)*: Book group has helped teach Noah how to be a good friend (without realizing it). As the kids have gotten older, their friendships have changed and they don't spend as much time together as they used to. But book club keeps Noah and me connected to these kids and their families, and it continues to be a safe place for Noah to build on those friendships.

Books will become a way to stay close as your kids get older.

Kristin *(Luci's mom)*: I originally joined the group because I was desperate for adult interaction, especially with adults whose kids were friends with my kid. Win-win! Now that the kids are teenagers and I don't see them as much as when they were little, I love that we have this book connection that will last forever!

Ann *(Dominic's mom)*: Now that my kid is a teenager and is gone more than he's home, it's great to have an activity to do together that doesn't take much time and keeps us connected.

Not to mention this will be a way to find and fall in love with books you may never have thought about and a way to introduce your old favorites to a new (and hopefully receptive) audience. All that accomplished in just a few hours each month!

Chapter 2

Creating Your Book Club

"The early summer

sky was the color

of cat vomit."

—opening of *Uglies*
by Scott Westerfield

Our kids were in kindergarten when we first started talking about forming a parent-child book club. The kids were already friends, we were becoming friends, and all of us loved reading. One of our founding members, Dana, was a middle school teacher and had done successful book clubs with her students. Another member, Michelle, was a children's book editor and author. Having some members with knowledge about children's books gave us the confidence to give it a go. But in hindsight, we now understand you don't actually need *any* expertise to start a group. All you need is a desire to read books with your kids and a willingness to try it.

Choosing the members of your book club is one of the most important decisions you will make in this process. You will be spending a lot of time and talking about very personal topics with the people in this group, possibly for years into the future. They will impact the kinds of books you read, the quality of your discussions, and the overall vibe of your group. So it's worth taking some time and thinking carefully about the other readers you invite along on the journey.

WHO TO INVITE?

When thinking about people who might be interested in starting a parent-child book club with you, here are some important factors to consider.

Your child's friends

Choosing families where your kids are already friends will certainly make the process easier. Kids are more likely to want to go to book club if they have friends who will be there. They are likely to stick with it longer if they look forward to hanging out with their friends once a month and talking books. That said, friendships change over time, and just because your kids are friends now doesn't mean they will stay close over the years. But book club can survive friendship changes. Every kid doesn't have to be friends with every other kid, but if each kid has a friend in the group, that is a big bonus.

Your friends

For the same reason that it's easier to start a book club with your child's friends, it is also easier to start a book club if *you* are friends (or hope to be friends) with the parents. You will spend a lot of time with the people in this group. It helps if you like each other. As with the kids, if each adult has a friend in the group, that's a good thing. If not, you will likely become friends over the course of book club.

Kids who like reading

This isn't a total prerequisite for starting a book club, but it does help if at least some of the kids are already book lovers. We had several kids in our group who didn't love to read or liked reading only a certain type of book. Some of those kids dropped out over time, but others stayed with the group for the long haul. Their enjoyment of reading certainly grew and broadened over the years, and they were exposed to new perspectives and books they never would have chosen on their own.

Proximity

Another suggestion, but not mandatory: It is much easier to go to book club if it's a short distance away. It's also easier to share books among members.

WHAT ABOUT DADS OR GRANDPARENTS?

Our book club happened to be all moms, but it certainly doesn't have to be that way. The only requirement for adult members is that they need to be excited about reading kids' books with their kid. That could easily be a dad, mom, grandma, grandpa, auntie, uncle, guardian, or even a family friend or neighbor. No matter who it is, they will no doubt find that participating in a book club with a special kid in their life is a great way to spend time together and develop a closer connection through books.

THE IMPORTANCE OF DIVERSITY AND REPRESENTATION

It's crucial to keep in mind that having people with a variety of viewpoints and experiences in your group will make your book club better. Think about that as you are deciding who to invite. Many Americans live in very segregated communities and don't have friends outside their own racial or ethnic group. So forming a book club with only your friends or families from your neighborhood may lead to a very homogenous group. If you have a homogenous friend group, consider

Owen

We formed our book club in Portland, Oregon, one of the whitest cities in the country. Our original group was all white and mostly boys. That certainly impacted the books we read in those early years—lots of white boy protagonists. Over the years our group evolved and became more diverse. When adding new members, we were intentional about bringing more girls into the group. Other kinds of diversity happened naturally.

We found that the more diverse our group got, the more interesting our conversations got. People from different backgrounds bring unique perspectives and life experiences to the group. They recommend different books to read. They fuel meaningful discussion, challenge commonly held beliefs, and bring new ideas. This doesn't mean you should seek out token representation. But it does mean that you should be aware of the communities your members are a part of, and that you should welcome members who are different from you.

inviting families from different friend groups, different communities, and with different experiences than your own. This will benefit your group in many, many ways—from the choice of books to the richness of your discussions. Of course, you should avoid "tokenism" (inviting someone from an underrepresented group just to give the appearance of diversity) or making a book club member feel that they are supposed to represent their cultural group or identity. See page 98 for more on how to create an inclusive atmosphere in your book club.

HOW MANY PEOPLE?

Another important decision to make is the number of adult-child pairs you invite into your book club. Size matters! The size of our book club fluctuated over the years. Our smallest group was ten people (five kids, five adults), and our biggest was eighteen people! We found that there are pros and cons to both.

Small group

The upside of having a smaller group is that it's easier to host the group in your home or other space. It's also easier to get through a meeting and for everyone to have a chance to participate and be heard. The downside is if a few people can't make the meeting, your group will be very small and can feel too quiet. Over the years, we decided the smallest meeting size that worked for us was three kids, three adults. If we couldn't

Dominic

At our meeting to discuss the book *1984*, we had just three kids and three adults show up. And yet I remember that being one of the best conversations we ever had in book club. There was lots of time to talk about the author's complex ideas, and everyone got to have their say.

reach that bar, we canceled the meeting. If you have a talkative bunch, though, perhaps that size is just right.

Big group

One advantage of having a bigger group is that meetings are livelier. With lots of people, there is never a lag in the conversation. Also, you are likely to have one or two families miss any given meeting (at least that's how it was in our group), so with a larger group you are guaranteed enough participants to have a good meeting.

There are a few challenges with a larger group, however. Fitting everyone in your home or other space is harder. Big groups take up a lot of room and need more chairs and snacks. With more members, each person has less opportunity to share their thoughts. Also, with more members in the rotation, you and your child will have fewer chances to pick the book the group reads. With twelve members, you each might get to choose just one book per year. Last, it can be more challenging to schedule meetings with a larger group—more people means more potential conflicts.

Sweet spot

Our group's ideal size was fourteen to sixteen members (seven or eight adult-child pairs). On the rare occasions when everyone shows up, you will have a full house and loud discussion. And you will likely never drop lower than three families at a meeting. For most meetings, you'll have ten to twelve people, which is the sweet spot. You are pretty much guaranteed a dynamic conversation with enough people sharing their ideas.

WHAT AGE TO START?

This is a good question, and the answer is easy: whenever you can. That said, we do think the elementary years (first through fifth grades) are the easiest time to start a book club. During these years, kids are just starting to read and

often love it, they still like hanging out with their parents, and adults have more control over their schedules. It's easier to lure them to book club with friends, snacks, and games.

But don't let the notion of "ideal" timing scare you off. We know people who started parent-child book clubs in middle school and even high school, and those worked too. The best time to start a book club with your kid is whenever you are ready to start it. Don't worry about whether it's the perfect time. Just do it!

CAN YOU START BEFORE YOUR CHILD IS READING INDEPENDENTLY?

Sure! If you have kids who are super excited about books and parents who are super excited to get a book club going, you can certainly start one before every member can read on their own. In that case, the parent needs to read the book aloud with their child or get the audiobook version. We had several members who did this during our first year of book club and it worked just fine. Eventually they transitioned to alternating who read each chapter until their children could read

independently. This was a great way to help those kids learn to read while keeping them in the book club.

HOW TO INVITE FAMILIES?

Once you've decided who you want to invite, it's time to reach out. Keep it simple. A short email outlining your desire is all it takes. Schedule a preliminary meeting with all interested families to discuss the details. At that first meeting you can choose the first book and set up a meeting calendar.

Here's the email Dana sent to parents in our original group all those years ago. It was short and to the point. She explained the overall idea and proposed a preliminary meeting. Meetings after that first one followed our meeting format, which is explained in detail in chapter 4.

Subject: book club with our kids?

Hi everyone,

Michelle and I have been discussing the idea of starting a parent/child book club. The basic idea is to get our kids together once a month to talk about a book that we have all read. We think it would be a lot of fun and hopefully get our kids even more excited about reading by giving them the opportunity to discuss what they are reading in a meaningful way.

We were thinking that we could introduce a new genre each month and recommend two or three books that we think would be fun to read. Then, our kids could vote on which book they want the group to read. Some genres we could read would be historical fiction, realism, adventure/survival, science fiction, graphic novels, fantasy, biography/autobiography, mystery, and nonfiction. In addition to reading the books, we would ask the kids (and perhaps the parents) to come prepared with something to share with the group—discussion questions, an illustration they've created based on the reading, a connection they made to the story, etc. It really would not be a lot of work, just something to share with the group.

What do you think?

We'd like to hold a pre-book club meeting to go over how it would work and to let the kids know what our first book will be. Normally we'll choose the book together, but for the first meeting we thought we'd pick the book. And, the book will be . . . *Harry Potter and the Sorcerer's Stone*! Michelle has offered to host the pre–book club meeting at her house on Monday.

If you think you might be interested, please come to the pre-meeting. We can all get together and figure out how we can make this work.

Sincerely, Dana

A FINAL WORD

Choosing the people to invite into your book club is a tricky step. It will have a big impact on which books you read, how your discussions go, and which friendships blossom. But the group is also likely to change and evolve over time. Do your best to find kids and adults that are a good match based on friendships, love of reading, and proximity to one another. Once you've settled on the members of your group, you can get into the fun stuff: planning your first meeting!

Chapter 3

Setting Up

"We carry with us,

as human beings,

not just the capacity to

be kind, but the very

choice of kindness."

—from *Wonder* by R. J. Palacio

Now that you know why it's good to start a family book club and you have some ideas about how to choose other families to start one with, it's time to think about the nuts and bolts of *how* to set up your meetings. The details can make all the difference in whether your meeting goes well and is fun, and whether the kids (and parents) want to come back. We tried a lot of different locations, snacks, and scheduling techniques before we figured out what worked best for us. We've included our tips and tricks in the following pages, but of course, what worked for us may not be the best fit for your group. Experiment and find the setup that works for you.

CHOOSING A BOOK

Before you have your meeting, you will need to choose the book your group will read. Choosing books is a *big* topic. Chapter 7 covers those details: which age categories to read, which genres, and how and where to find great books.

Chapters 8 through 11 are chock-full of recommended booklists (including the one hundred our book club read together), and the Resources section on page 198 features websites to help you find even more.

WHO PICKS THE BOOKS— KIDS OR ADULTS?

Right off the bat you will need to decide *who* will choose the books for your book club. Will it be the adults or the kids? Like so many things in our book club, this element changed for us over time.

Adults Choose

For the first few years of our group, when the kids were very young, the adults chose the books. Sometimes we chose one book we thought they might like or would make for an interesting discussion. More often we chose a genre, like fantasy or mystery, then gave the kids two or three options to choose from within that genre. The kids voted on which one they wanted to read next. Our reasoning was that if we let the kids choose the books completely on their own, we would end up reading *Diary of a Wimpy Kid* and the Warriors cat series month after month. (In first grade, those were some of their favorite books, and we *did* read them in our book club. But we also read a lot of other amazing books.)

One of the benefits of adults choosing is that the kids end up reading books they wouldn't otherwise choose, such as books written in earlier eras or about characters and settings that are totally unfamiliar to them. When the parents choose the books, it also gives you a chance to pick stories with specific topics and themes that you want to discuss with your kids. For example, if something is going on at school or with some of the kids in your group, you might choose to read about it so that you can talk about it in a more relaxed way. Book club can be a great place to have those conversations about difficult issues.

Adults *and* Kids Choose

We soon discovered that if we adults chose *all* the books, the kids lost interest. It's important for the kids in your group to have agency and to feel like it's their book club too. They will be much more likely to enjoy book club and want to keep going if they and

their friends are picking at least some of the books.

You could try alternating months that are "kid pick" and "adult pick." (Unfortunately, for our group, with twelve members, this meant that each kid got to choose just one book per year.)

You could also put the host family in charge of selecting the book. The host kid *or* host parent can choose the book, depending on which of them had something in mind, or the pair can work together to choose their book. This method of choosing is nice because if one of you doesn't have a great book in mind, the other usually does. Or, if one of you picked the last few books in that family pair, then it's the other person's turn. Each family pair gets to work it out among themselves.

Kids Choose

If we had let our kids choose all the books starting when they were in first grade, we would have read very different books for those first few years. And that probably would have been OK. We might have missed some of the historical fiction or award-winning books that we read, but we would have gotten a good glimpse into our kids' favorite books. Kids picking the books could work well for some groups.

During the high school years and into college, as our kids became young adults, we gave them full control of choosing the books. We noticed that as they got older, they chose better books with meatier things to discuss. The books they selected in the last few years of our book club were excellent—at least as good as the books we chose when they were younger.

There are many ways to decide who will pick the books. Flexibility is the key! Discuss and try different methods that give your kids some agency and

ownership, while also bringing variety to your reading list. Eventually you'll hit on what works best for your group.

GETTING THE BOOK

Getting enough copies of the book for everyone, all at the same time, can be a challenge. The library has limited copies and popular books often have long hold lines. You don't want the expense of having to buy books to be a barrier for families who want to participate. Here are a couple of tricks and resources to get the books you need without breaking the bank.

Choose older books

Try *not* to pick brand-new books or current bestsellers. Older books are easier to get at the library. Publishers usually release a book in hardcover first, then some months or years later they release the paperback version, which is cheaper if members want to buy a copy. (And if you do end up buying a copy, buy from your local, independent bookstore!) Also note that "older" doesn't have to mean "old"—the further back you go, the less diverse the books get. By "older," we mean old enough to be out in paperback or less popular at the library.

Share copies

Share books between members! When one family finishes a book, they pass it on to another family. With a month between books, there is usually time for two families to read each book.

Library books

Check out older books from your local library or your kids' school libraries. Remember, if you have multiple library cards (yours, your kids', your partner's) then you can check out multiple copies and share them with the group.

Used books

As long as the book isn't brand-new, you can usually find a few cheaper used copies. Look for used bookstores in your town, or check online used booksellers (see Resources, page 198).

Digital and audiobooks

These can be a less expensive option than buying a print book. You may also be able to borrow the digital or audio version from your library.

READING SUPPLIES

Here are a couple of items that are nice for kids (and adults too) to have on hand while reading.

Notebook

Every kid in our group had a spiral notebook that they used for book club. As they read the books, they used their notebook to write down discussion and trivia questions. This is also where they drew pictures inspired by the books and wrote down their book ratings (see pages 51 to 54 in chapter 4). Not only was this a good place to keep everything organized, but it's fun to have a record of all the books we read and to see how the kids' questions and drawings changed over the years. In our group, only the kids had notebooks, but there's no reason why parents couldn't have a notebook of their own.

Sticky notes

It's good to have sticky notes on hand when reading the book so you can mark sections that may make for good discussion or trivia questions. You can also mark sections you found interesting and want to read aloud to the group. If you have sticky notes in a variety of colors, you can use yellow for discussion, green for trivia, and so on.

LOCATION

The next step in holding your first book club is choosing the location for the meeting. In our group, the person hosting the book club also picked the location. Although our meetings were often held in our homes, over the years we met in a variety of places. Some of us have smaller homes, where it was a challenge to host a large group. And sometimes other siblings or rowdy dogs can make meetings at home less than ideal. Here are some options to try out.

PLACES YOU CAN MEET FOR BOOK CLUB:

- *Your home*

- *Local park*

- *School playground*

- *Community center: Many community centers have rooms you can reserve for meetings.*

- *Library: Many libraries have rooms you can reserve for meetings.*

- *Coffee shop or restaurant: Pick a time when it won't be too busy, so the staff doesn't mind if you're there for a while. Ordering food and drinks can also buy some good will.*

- *Online: You can host a virtual meeting on platforms such as Zoom, Skype, or Google Hangouts.*

We tried all of these! When our kids were younger they went to the same school, so sometimes we would meet after school at the playground. After a half hour of the kids running around, we would gather together at the picnic table for snacks and our book discussion. For our book club on *The Fault in Our Stars*, we went to see the movie in the theater together and afterward discussed the book in a coffee shop next to the theater. And when we were confined to our homes and practicing social distancing during the coronavirus pandemic of 2020, we held our book club meetings virtually, on Zoom.

VIRTUAL BOOK CLUB MEETINGS:

Dana

In March of 2020, our kids were seniors looking forward to prom, graduation, and their last days with their high school friends. Then the COVID-19 pandemic hit. Although there were plenty of losses and disappointments during this time, one ray of sunshine was that they suddenly had extra time on their hands and were able to read books for pleasure again. A lot of books. For those five months before college, we held our book club meetings virtually, using Zoom.

For the first time in a long time, no one had a conflict and all were able to attend. It was great to see everyone online and to be able to catch up and spend a few hours together. During our first virtual meeting, we quickly realized that someone needed to act as the facilitator to keep people from talking over each other and to ensure that quieter members were able to contribute. But once we got the system down, the rest of our meetings flowed smoothly. Although we prefer meeting in person, we discovered that virtual meetings are a great alternative. And the next time someone is unable to make it to book club because they are on a family vacation, or home sick with a cold, they will have the option of joining book club virtually. A quarantine silver lining!

MEETING SUPPLIES

You really don't need to have much on hand when you host a book club meeting. This part of the setup can be as simple or as complex as you want. But there are a few items that will make meeting participation a little easier:

Copies of the Book

All members of the book club should bring their own copy of the book to the meeting. If the host has extra copies, it's nice to have those available in case someone forgets theirs or borrowed it from someone else. That way when you are debating the correct answer to a trivia question, the kids can use the book to back up their answers.

Pens/Pencils and Scrap Paper

Have writing materials available to make notes and play games. Sometimes people won't have written down their trivia questions before the meeting, so having pens and paper at the ready makes it easier for them to jot those down during free time. We also used scrap paper to keep track of the responses to the trivia questions and, most important, to keep score so we knew who won!

Bookmark Bonanza!

We know of another book club that handed out bookmarks at the end of each meeting. The bookmarks were printed with the title of the next book to be read, as well as the date and location of the next meeting! This group was *way* more organized and ambitious than we were.

FOOD

Before our first meeting, while we were still in the planning stage, we had grand visions of the host providing dinner for everyone. "We'll have a night off from cooking!" we thought happily. We quickly realized this put too much pressure on the host. Different allergies and food preferences alone made it a huge challenge. We debated doing it potluck-style, where everyone would bring something, or even just ordering a pizza. In the end, we decided to keep our meetings easy and not make our lives more hectic than they already were. We realized that serving snacks worked best for us.

The host provided a few healthy snacks and drinks, and other families brought stuff to add if they wanted. If there were sweets, we saved those until the end of the meeting to avoid sugar highs while discussing the book. We timed our meetings so they didn't fall during meal times.

This food decision kept things easy for us. However, if you or your families love to cook, you might have a lot of fun adding a meal to your meetings. Go for it!

EASY, HEALTHY SNACK IDEAS:

- *Hummus and veggies*
- *Chips and salsa*
- *Cheese and crackers*
- *Yogurt-covered pretzels*
- *Popcorn*
- *Fruit (apples, clementines, and grapes)*
- *Smoothies*

Place the food in the middle of wherever the group will be sitting and talking. This ensures that people don't constantly wander off during the conversation to refill their plates in the kitchen.

If you're feeling ambitious, it can be fun to serve food that is associated with or mentioned in the book you are reading. In the book *The Radius of Us*, one of the main characters loves pupusas, thick corn cakes stuffed with

Owen

Food is a good way to keep people happy while at book club. But there is a fine line between a beneficial supplement to the enjoyment of all members and a flat-out distraction. In general, snacks are best when they are simple, neat, and not prone to making fingers sticky. Snacks that can be eaten easily will keep kids happy, without distracting a member from actually participating in the discussion. If you decide to serve a meal at book club, it is best to eat the meal before you start your discussion to avoid the food being the main focus for hungry children.

savory filling, which is the national dish of El Salvador. When we met to discuss this book, one of our families brought pupusas from a local food cart to share. This was a huge hit with the group, and it helped us make a connection with the character from the story. (More on book-inspired food on page 66.)

CLEAN UP

From our very first meeting we established a "no cleaning necessary" rule so the host did not feel pressure to spend more time cleaning their home than they normally would. We highly recommend instating this policy! The last thing you want to do is put up barriers to hosting. Keep it casual.

Once you are finished talking about the book, everyone should pitch in and help clean up. If you can designate the last five to ten minutes as group cleanup time, that makes it less work for the host. Cleanup is a great time to chat casually again before you leave. This creates a nice bookend of social time during the meetings: There's time to chat while you set up for the meeting and during the cleanup afterward.

SCHEDULING

One of the last tasks is scheduling the next meeting. This can be a big challenge for book clubs. It certainly was for our group, especially as our kids got older and more involved with other activities. Trying to find a time that works for everyone can feel like a Herculean task. Between school, extracurricular activities, holidays, and family commitments, it seems like there's never a good time to meet. Over the years, we tried a variety of methods to handle scheduling.

A Set Meeting Time

Try picking a day and time that will generally work for the group and sticking to it every month. Maybe it's the last Friday afternoon of the month, or the first Saturday morning of the month. The time is set and you meet then, even if some members are not available. We had set meetings like this where only three kids were available, and even though it was a small, intimate group, we still had great discussions.

One advantage to this system is that everyone always knows when the next meeting will be. If you are planning a trip six months in the future, you can take into account when the book club is scheduled to meet. Obviously, the drawback with this system is that typically at least one family ends up having a conflict and has to miss the meeting.

Pick a Date That Works for Everyone

Another method is coordinating a meeting time that works for everyone each month (or however often you

decide to meet). For every meeting, several days and times are suggested, and the group votes on a time that works best for the most people (and the host, of course). The advantage to this method is that when it works, no one gets left out. The disadvantage is that it can take a while to find a date that works for everyone.

The Host Sets the Date

This method falls somewhere in between the two methods described above. The host picks a date and time that works best for them, taking into account what works for most of the group. The advantage to this method is that it is faster and easier to find a date that works for most, though not necessarily all, of the group.

Establish a Rotation

You wouldn't think deciding who's next to host and choose the book would be so hard to figure out. But it is! At least, it was for us. We struggled with it in the beginning, but eventually we established a rotation based on first names in alphabetical order. You could also try rotating the hosting

and book-choosing responsibilities by birthday, or draw names out of a hat.

Choose the Next Book

The person choosing the next book may already know what they want to read. If they do, tell the group during scheduling time so everyone has time to get the book. If they don't know what they want to read yet, have them email the group in the next few days. Everyone needs enough time to get ahold of the book and read it, especially if parent and child are sharing one copy.

ELECT A COMMUNICATION CAPTAIN

After each meeting, someone needs to send a message to the group. This can be an email or a text. For our group, this message included a brief summary of the most recent meeting and general impressions of the book. It also reminded us who was hosting next and, most important, what book we would be reading. The responsibility of this communication can fall to the person who just hosted or the person hosting next. Or, you can pick one person to always take on this task.

SAMPLE EMAIL FROM OUR COMMUNICATION CAPTAIN

Hey All,

For those of you who were unable to make our last meeting, we discussed *This Time Will Be Different* by Misa Sugiura. Overall the book was well received, and it sparked an interesting discussion about race, Japanese internment camps, and how injustices of the past can have long-lasting impacts. Thanks for hosting, Linda and Elena!

For our next book, Luci and I have picked a YA thriller called *Monday's Not Coming* by Tiffany D. Jackson. There are copies available at the library, and we are happy to share our copy when we finish reading.

Below is a Doodle poll link for picking our next meeting date.

Thanks! Kristin

ADAPTING AS KIDS GET OLDER

At the start of middle school, and again at the start of high school, we asked the kids if they were still interested in continuing with the book club or if they were ready to quit. We parents wanted to make sure the group was something *they* wanted to continue. We didn't want to force them or have to nag them to do it. We did lose a member or two at each of these junctures, but it ensured that the kids who continued did so because they wanted to.

The kids' attachment to book club surprised us. When they were juniors in high school we were meeting every six weeks. We parents suggested that we meet less often, maybe every couple of months, so they would have enough time for all their other stuff.

Ronan

There have been a few times in book club where we read a book that was assigned in school. This is really helpful because you get a chance to do your homework and read the book club book at the same time. Reading a book for both also gives you a deeper understanding of the material because you talk about different things in book club versus at school.

They rejected our proposal soundly and made a countersuggestion: They wanted to meet *more* often! We bumped it back up to our earlier once-a-month schedule!

As the kids' schedules get busier, one trick is to pick books they have to read for school. *The Outsiders, To Kill a Mockingbird*, and *Lord of the Flies* were all books we read that were also assigned to at least some of the kids in our group. The books were interesting to discuss and we killed two birds with one stone.

As the kids got older, they also took more ownership of the group. Not only did they pick the books, but they also led our discussions. (We parents still helped with scheduling and emails—and snacks, of course!) Another thing that changed for our group was that not everyone read the book every month. Sometimes just the kids and the one parent who was hosting read the book. Sometimes a kid read the first couple of chapters and decided it wasn't for them, but they still came to chat about it. As teenagers, the kids should have total freedom to decide if they don't want to read the book because they are just not interested in the topic, or because they are buried in writing their college application essays! This kept book club in the "fun activity" category all those years; it never felt like an extra chore the kids had to do.

Your kids will inevitably have their own competing passions and commitments, but if you can be flexible with your book club's rules and structure and check in with your kids often, you will have a better chance of keeping it going for many years.

A FINAL WORD

As you can see, a lot more goes into creating a successful, sustainable book club than just reading the same book together. If you take some time as you are forming your book club to decide how to set up your meetings, you will have a good foundation in place—a foundation that can carry you happily along for many years and through many books.

HOW BOOK CLUB HAS CHANGED FOR US:

Noah

The length and quality of our discussions have gone up as we have grown older. Early on, everyone would share discussion questions, which would spark a few comments and opinions lasting about fifteen minutes. Our attention spans just couldn't sustain a discussion for much longer than that. Our parents did a lot to facilitate even those shorter discussions. Now, we sometimes have discussions that last an hour without any adult contributions. Just one good question can get us talking for an hour or more. The discussions have become a much bigger part of our meetings.

Dominic

When we first started our book club, we spent an hour before the book discussion having what we called "Fun Time"—playing basketball, foosball, air hockey . . . whatever games the host had. As we have gotten older, that "Fun Time" hasn't gone away, but it has taken a different form. Now, we use that time before the book discussion to catch up with old friends. Some of us go to different high schools and have drifted apart a bit. If it weren't for book club, we wouldn't have that chance to talk and stay connected.

Chapter 4
The Meeting

"Sometimes it seemed to him that his life was delicate as a dandelion. One little puff from any direction, and it was blown to bits."

—from *Bridge to Terabithia* by Katherine Paterson

Creating a meeting structure that works for your group is probably the most important thing you can do to ensure its success and longevity. It's worth taking the time to think, talk, and plan ahead. This chapter shows you exactly what *we* did in our book club—what worked for us. It also gives you a sense of what different models offer, so you can decide what structure works best for you and your kids, depending on their ages. Read on, and then use these ideas to brainstorm with the adults and kids in your book club.

Once you figure out what structure sounds good, try it for a few meetings. See how it goes. If it doesn't work for your group, adapt. Change things. Try something new.

OUR MEETING STRUCTURE

Fun Time: 30–60 minutes

Book Rating: 5 minutes

Book Drawing: 5 minutes

Trivia: 15 minutes

Book Discussion: 30 minutes

Wrap-Up: 5 minutes

FUN TIME

We started our book club when the kids were in first grade. Sure, the parents wanted to encourage the kids to read more, but we also wanted to give them a chance to socialize outside of school and strengthen their brand-new friendships. And we were hoping to create a regular time and place to get to know each other better.

From the very beginning, we decided to add in some unstructured time at the start of each meeting, and we continued it throughout the years. It was always thirty to sixty minutes long, depending on how much time everyone had for that particular meeting. When the kids were younger, this was their time to run around screaming like banshees, to play and have fun together. It was also the time for us parents to share a drink and chat about work, school, parenting, whatever.

The kids dubbed this part of book club "Fun Time," and the name stuck. Fun Time served another important purpose when the kids were little—after running around for a while, they could more easily sit in one spot for an hour and talk about books. Without Fun Time, that would have been tough. Also during Fun Time, we parents were able to get stuff ready for the meeting, setting out snacks, pens, and paper while we caught up. Last, anyone who didn't do their trivia or discussion questions yet could do it during Fun Time.

As your kids become better friends, they won't need any help thinking of stuff to do during Fun Time. But for those first few meetings you might pull out some balls, Lego bricks, or other toys that encourage group play. Good outside games include tag, kick-the-can, and hide-and-seek. Pick something that requires them to move their bodies since there will be a lot of sitting during the rest of the meeting.

Even as the kids grew into teenagers, began high school, and eventually approached graduation, we still had Fun Time at the start of every book club. Of course, they stopped playing hide-and-seek, but they still went off on their own to hang out. Many of them weren't in the same social groups at school, and some went to different schools. They didn't see each other every day, so they always had a lot to catch up on.

So did the grown-ups. Sometimes we joined in on the kid conversations and sometimes we did our own thing. (And "our own thing" usually involved wine.)

BOOK RATING

As soon as we sat down to start the actual book club meeting, the first thing we did was rate the book. Each person (kids and parents) ranked the book on a scale of one to ten, with one

Luci

When we were little, Fun Time was just us running around in someone's backyard playing games like soccer, basketball, or kickball. At my house we always played in our tree house. As we got older, Fun Time shifted to the basements, where we played ping-pong, foosball, or air hockey.

For me, Fun Time has always been a chance to bond with the other kids in book club. Even now, it's always nice to have that time to catch up with friends I haven't seen or talked to in a while. It's also nice not to jump straight into talking about our book.

being awful and ten being awesome, and took about a minute to explain *why* they gave it that rating. What did we like or not like about the book?

Each person can say their rating aloud, but we discovered that when the kids were a certain age (middle school) they all pretty much parroted whatever the first person said about the book. Or if someone had a very strong opinion about the book, the rest followed suit. Sometimes, at certain ages, kids are too shy to tell their peers what they really think.

If the same is true for your kids (if, say, they're in middle school), do your book ratings anonymously. For example, for many years, we each wrote our number and thoughts on a slip of paper and one person read them all aloud. (Once our kids got older, they had *no problem* voicing their own independent opinions. In fact, they relished arguing about the merits of the books we read together, so we stopped the anonymous ratings.)

The most important part of Book Rating is talking about *why* you did or didn't like the book. This is a perfect time to talk about writing techniques the author used—character development, world building, story arc—and

whether they are effective or not. Some questions you might ask:

- *Does the beginning of the book pull you in? Is it confusing?*

- *Does the start of the book make you want to keep reading?*

- *Are the dialogue and characters believable?*

- *Does the world feel real?*

- *Is there enough detail? Too much?*

- *Does the plot stay on course and pull you toward the climax?*

- *Or does it veer off on tangents or drag in the middle?*

- *Does the climax feel climactic enough?*

- *Is the end of the story, the resolution, satisfying?*

- *Which plot elements are wrapped up and which are left unfinished? Why?*

- *What do you think of the author's Voice, with a capital V? Is it unique?*

Rating the books is a great way to get everyone transitioned from Fun Time to Book Discussion time. Book Rating helps us ease everyone into the conversation, and explaining ratings helps launch the conversation into a more interesting book discussion, since you've already started to think about the themes and topics of the book.

Noah

Not everyone loves every book and usually there is a wide range of perspectives and tastes. Sometimes listening to someone else's rating and explanation changes your perspective and makes you realize something about the book you didn't think of before.

Sometimes it can be nerve-racking, however, to put your rating out there when you know your friends might disagree. It's a show of bravery and confidence to share your rating, especially when it's different from everyone else's. We have some heated debates about book ratings, but in the end we respect each other's perspectives because they are thoughtful.

BOOK DRAWING

The kids came up with this activity, and it's always been one of the most fun and funny parts of our meeting. Basically, each kid does a drawing (at home) inspired by the book we read. Parents can certainly do the book drawings as well, but our group was filled with art-phobic adults. Some kids take a long time doing intricate, detailed, beautiful illustrations; others spend seconds on it. The drawing can be a character, a scene, or even an abstract idea. During the Book Drawing part of the meeting, each person shows their drawing and the rest of the group tries to guess what it is. It's harder than you think!

Books offer a unique art opportunity because each reader forms their own ideas about what the world and characters look like. Drawing from a book allows you to share *your* interpretation of the author's words. At the beginning of our book club, we gave each kid a blank book club notebook (see Reading Supplies, page 37), where they could do their drawings and write their trivia and discussion questions. After eleven years and one hundred books, our kids have notebooks showing a full history of all the books we've read together, which is pretty cool.

Owen

Book Drawing has always been my favorite part of book club. Today I have multiple book club notebooks, each full of drawings that show the progression of my art. What I've chosen to draw over the years has changed a lot. When I was younger I liked drawing a scene that would be difficult for people to guess. As I got older, I began to care less about stumping people and focused more on the actual art. Now I often don't even draw a specific scene from the book. Instead, I try to capture a theme or the general essence of the book. When we read *A Separate Peace*, I drew a tree that has a pivotal role in setting up the story. Here is the very first drawing I did for our very first book club when we discussed *Harry Potter and the Sorcerer's Stone*, as well as a drawing I did a few years later of the final battle scene in *Ready Player One*.

TRIVIA

Book Drawing will work in your group if your kids enjoy art, but no one should be forced to draw if they don't like it. The kids in our group enjoyed drawing through the middle school years, but once they started high school they pretty much dropped this activity—except for our resident book club artist, Owen, who has done a drawing for all one hundred books we've read.

Another element of our book club structure that has been there since the first meeting is the trivia contest. We decided to include a trivia game because we thought it might encourage us—parents included—to read the books carefully, not just skim them. We are also a pretty competitive group who loves games, so we figured we'd enjoy it. We were right. Today it's still one of the most popular parts of book club, especially for the kids.

Here's how the trivia contest works: Each parent and kid comes to the meeting with two to four trivia questions. If you don't have time to write them ahead of the meeting, it's easy to write a few during Fun Time. Here are a few sample trivia questions from past book clubs.

- *What kind of cheese gives you the "cheese touch" in* Diary of a Wimpy Kid?

- *What tattoos does Karou have on her hands in* Daughter of Smoke & Bone?

- *What type of wood is Harry Potter's wand made of?*

We split into two teams. Our teams were *always* kids versus parents, but you can create whatever teams you want. Each team alternates asking a trivia question and then answering one. Each trivia question is worth one point and a scorekeeper tallies up the points. Whichever team has more points at the end of the questions is the winner. In our book club, Kid Team usually crushed Parent Team, but occasionally parents got a surprise victory.

The trivia game is a lot of fun and gets everyone laughing, but it accomplishes something deeper as well. Over the years the kids have expressed how much it has helped them learn to read books more carefully and remember details—an important skill for high school English.

One Trivia pitfall to avoid: Beware of impossible-to-answer questions

Dominic

My favorite part of book club has always been the trivia game, because it's simple and competitive. It also helped us hone our skills for Battle of the Books, a reading competition for kids in grades three through twelve that takes place in all fifty states (see Resources, page 198). It's like a spelling bee or chess match, but for books! When competing in Battle of the Books you have a team of four kids who must read sixteen books chosen by your state. After months of reading those books (sometimes multiple times), your team competes in trivia matches—first within your own school, then against winning teams from other schools around your state. Members of our book club formed a team in third grade. We quickly learned we had an advantage over other teams: We'd been practicing our trivia skills for two years in book club. Our team did very well throughout elementary school, winning our grade, school, and eventually district and state matches. By middle school we'd had enough of "competitive reading" and went back to reading purely for fun.

that focus on specific pages of the book as opposed to specific moments or characters. Dominic was the king of these, posing doozies like, "How many times does the author use the word *I* on pages 67 through 84?" No one will be able to answer these kinds of questions. Depending on how competitive your group is, you may or may not need to set some rules about the kinds of questions you can ask.

BOOK DISCUSSION

At last, we are at the meat and potatoes of the meeting: Book Discussion. This is when we actually talk about the

important, interesting elements of the book we all read: the characters and the choices they made, ethical dilemmas, themes, author voice and abilities, connections to current events, and so on. The way our group structures that discussion is a question-and-answer format. Each member comes to the meeting with two to four discussion questions. We use those questions to launch into a pretty freewheeling group discussion. Anyone can pose their question at any time, but if no one chimes in or if one person is asking most of the questions, an adult steps in to call on people in turn.

Coming in with good questions is what makes for a good discussion. And having a good discussion is what book club is *all about*. The ease of coming up with good discussion questions definitely depends on the quality of the book you're reading. Some books have a plethora of ethical dilemmas, bad choices by the narrator, and deeper societal issues that make it easy to come up with juicy questions. But sometimes plot-driven books can be difficult to discuss if there isn't much deeper stuff going on beneath the action.

The best discussion questions are:

Open-ended

You shouldn't be able to answer a discussion question with a simple *yes* or *no* or one-word answer. For example, a bad discussion question for *Hatchet* would be, "Did you like the shelter Brian built?" A good discussion question would be, "What would you do if you were lost in the wilderness like Brian?"

Spark debate

If everyone has the same response to a question, the discussion is boring. You want questions that will elicit different responses from different people. Something like, "Do you think young people would do a better job of running the world than adults right now, or would it be like *Lord of the Flies*?" is sure to start an interesting conversation, especially between kids and parents.

Personal

It's fascinating to learn more about your friends and your kids through their answers to questions like, "Have you ever been bullied or seen bullying

like in *Wonder*? What did you do? What do you wish you'd done?"

In our group, discussion questions always come *after* the trivia game. The first few years of book club we did our discussion before the trivia game, but discovered that our discussion questions often ruined the trivia by giving away answers. So we switched the order. Doing the trivia before the discussion is also helpful because sometimes a trivia question will remind you of something you forgot about in the book and give you another topic to bring up during discussion.

Coming up with thoughtful, engaging discussion questions isn't always easy, but it's absolutely necessary for a fun,

Ronan

I think the book discussion is [the] most important part of book club. A good way to find material for your discussion questions is to consider a character's thoughts and actions. If you disagreed with something they did in the story, you can ask something like, "What would you do in that situation?" or "How would the story be different if that character made a different choice?" These kinds of questions relate the book to your own life, make people think, and are interesting to talk about.

interesting book club. With practice it will become second nature.

DISCUSSION QUESTIONS FOR ANY BOOK

Can't think of a discussion question? Here are some samples that will work for nearly any book.

- *What did you like about this book?*

- *What did you dislike about this book?*

- *Who is telling this story (who's the narrator)?*

- *Who was your favorite character and why?*

- *What did you think of the choices the main character made?*

- *What do you think would have happened if that character made a different choice?*

- *What would you do if you were in the main character's position?*

- *Did anything happen in the story that reminded you of your own life?*

- *Do you have anything in common with a character in the story?*

- *What was your favorite part of the story and why?*

- *What was the funniest part of the story?*

- *What was the saddest part of the story?*

- *Was the plot believable?*

- *Were the characters realistic?*

- *Did the beginning of the story pull you in?*

- *Was the end of the story satisfying?*

- *What would you have done differently if you were the author?*

- *How could the author make this a better book?*

- *What do you think the author was trying to tell us with this story?*

- *Whose voice(s) is/are highlighted or privileged in this story? Who do we never hear from? What might this mean about the author's worldview/biases?*

- *How are our responses to this story or characters shaped by our own worldview/biases?*

WRAP-UP

At the end of the meeting there are four crucial things to figure out before everyone heads home. Chapter 3 has information about how to do each of these steps. You should decide:

- Who *will choose the next book.*

- What *the next book will be.*

- When *the next meeting will be.*

- Where *the next meeting will be.*

If the next host isn't sure about these four questions, they should email the group in the next few days. This future-meeting conversation is a good way to transition out of your book discussion and into ideas for your next book. If the next book chooser doesn't know what book they want to do next, this is a good time to brainstorm book ideas as a group. Part 2 of this book shows you how to choose great titles.

Check out our many lists of recommended books and be inspired!

A FINAL WORD

Remember, this is just how we structured *our* book club meetings. Your meeting structure needs to work for your group. We chose these elements because they were the things we all—parents *and* kids—enjoyed. We suspect that some of them will work well in any book club, but it's up to your group what you do and when and how you do it.

Be creative!

Chapter 5 will give you some additional ideas to try. There are some activities we tried in our group that ended up not working for us, as well as some ideas we've heard about from other book clubs. The only thing that's mandatory for your meeting: Make sure it's fun for everyone!

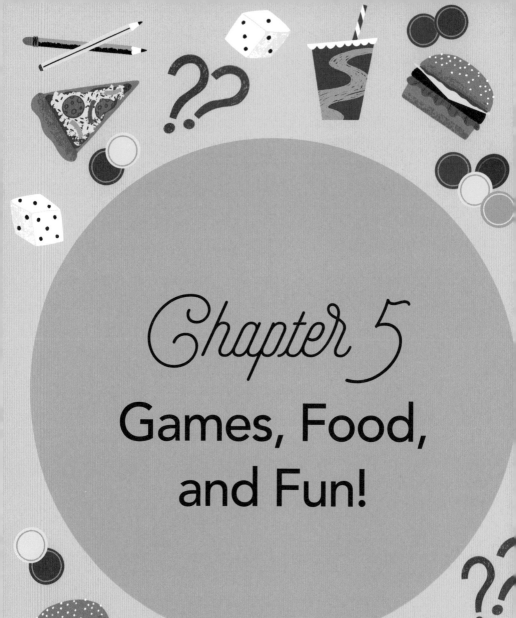

Chapter 5
Games, Food, and Fun!

"We went to the moon to have fun, but the moon turned out to completely suck."

—from *Feed* by M. T. Anderson

There are so many things you can do to make your book club fun and playful. You can dress up in costumes based on book characters. You can cook and eat foods from the book. You can do book-related crafts and games. The options are never-ending.

In this chapter you will find ideas for how to bring more fun to your book club. What you choose to do depends entirely on what your group is like. If you've got crafters and knitters, do some crafting and knitting! If you've got drama people, play charades and act out scenes from the book! If you're like us and have busy, tired adults who look forward to book club as a chance to relax and spend time with friends, then do that.

We want to preface this chapter with this: It's completely OK to do *no extra activities at all*. That's fine! Really! Being in a book club with your kid, reading books with them month after month, is enough. Do *not* feel pressure to take on extra work beyond that. In our book club we opted for sticking with what worked for us and was easy; we didn't put pressure on ourselves to do more.

We interviewed a few other parent-child book club organizers—Pam, Meg, Kendra, and Tasha—about their cool book-themed activities, crafts, and food. One book club made a book-related dinner for every meeting! Another club staged a book-inspired whodunnit mystery for the kids to solve. If this is who you are and it comes naturally and easily to your group, that's fabulous. Knock yourself out. But don't let it overwhelm you or lead to the demise of your club because it's not sustainable. Keep in mind that the goal of book club is fostering a love of reading and finding a community of people centered on books. Anything you do beyond that is gravy.

GAMES

Games are a great way to keep kids (especially younger kids) engaged at meetings. Few kids have the attention span for an hour-long book discussion. Adding a game to your meeting routine is an easy way to add some fun. Here are some games that work in a book club setting.

Trivia

A trivia game can take many forms. Each member can come up with a few questions, or the host can write all the questions. You can break into teams, taking turns asking questions to the other team. Or the host can ask all the questions for the two teams. Once the questions are finished, the team with the most correct answers wins. Or, if you want to play every person for themselves, each member can ask their questions to the whole group and whoever gets the most correct wins.

Trivia was our book club's favorite game for eleven years. (In chapter 4, you will find a detailed description of how we played during our meetings—see page 54). We found it helpful to assign one person the job of keeping track of the points. We also required that each player mark the answer to their trivia question in the book, in case a dispute needed settling. (No, we are not competitive at all. Why would you think that?) In our trivia games, you could earn a full point or partial points if you got part of the question right.

WE LOVE TRIVIA!

Ronan

Trivia is one of the oldest traditions in our book club. We've done it at every meeting for the past eleven years. We tried other games, but this is the one we've liked the most. In the beginning it was always kids versus grown-ups, and we kids took beating them *very* seriously. We kept track of points and even awarded half or quarter points for multipart questions. Trivia has gotten less competitive over the years. We no longer have teams and we don't care so much about who wins. I don't think this shift happened because we're less competitive (I, for one, am more competitive now, not less). I think we've realized that the important part of book club is not knowing a bunch of random facts about the book; it's about understanding the deeper themes and having a good discussion. That said, we still like playing trivia and do it at every meeting.

Catchphrase

In this game, everyone writes down character names, places, objects, or anything related to the book you've read on little slips of paper, then folds and tosses them in a hat. Each member should write down two or three clues (that way you have enough for everyone to take a few turns). Divide into teams. Then, taking turns, each person pulls a slip of paper out of the hat and has a short amount of time (we set our timer to thirty seconds) to describe the word on their paper without saying the actual word, while their team tries to guess what the word is. When their team guesses the word correctly or time runs out, it switches to the other team. When the slips of paper are gone, the team with the most points wins.

Charades

This game is similar to Catchphrase. Everyone writes down character names, places, objects, or anything related to the book you've read on little slips of paper, then folds and tosses them in a hat. Team up, then a player from one team draws a slip of paper

and *silently* acts out the word for their team. No talking. The rest of the team has a designated amount of time to guess right to score a point. Then the other team goes and you take turns until all the words are used. The team with the most points at the end wins.

Pictionary

This game is the same as charades, except the player draws a picture instead of acting out the word. Other teammates try to guess the book-related word they are drawing.

Bingo

This is a good game for younger kids and for those who like more luck-based games. Before the meeting, the host writes a bunch of book-related words on slips of paper and puts them in a hat. Then go to one of the many free bingo card generator websites, type in all the words, and print the bingo cards for each player. During the meeting, the host pulls words from the hat and players cover their squares until someone completes a line. Players can cross out words with a pen, or if you want to play multiple times, cut up some blank paper tokens ahead of time that players can use to cover the squares.

COSTUMES AND FOOD

Everyone loves dressing up and eating delicious snacks! Transport your group to Hogwarts with wands, butter (root) beer, and Bertie Bott's Every Flavor Beans. Immerse yourselves in the Hunger Games by dressing up for the "reaping." Serve dragon cupcakes in honor of Toothless the dragon. There is nothing better than seeing a group of second graders and grown-ups wearing Viking hats. The possibilities are endless!

Besides being just plain fun, book-themed costumes and food can help kids relate to the characters and settings, and they can add more depth to your discussion. Dressing up as Ponyboy from *The Outsiders* helps you relate to his plight. Eating bangers and mash can create just the right atmosphere for a rousing discussion about a book set in England. Adding these elements will undoubtedly create excitement about going to book club and will encourage kids to read and absorb the book. Don't, however, feel like these extras need to be a regular part of your book club. If you do them once or twice a year, they will feel more special (and less stressful for the hosts).

A Note about Costumes and Food

When adding book-related costumes and food to your meeting, here are a few rules of thumb.

BE SENSITIVE. Cultures are not costumes. Book clubs should never encourage costumes that involve cultural denigration or appropriation. Dressing up with the best intentions in the wrong "costumes" can be insulting, offensive, or even traumatizing to some members of the group. Even if nobody in your group is offended, it is never appropriate to dress in a manner that is racist, bigoted, xenophobic, sexist, or homophobic. Before your group does a cosplay meeting, have a discussion about when costumes have the potential to cause harm.

BE INCLUSIVE. Dressing up in costumes and preparing food for the whole group takes time and money. While some families might love to make elaborate cakes or intricate outfits, others may barely have time to make dinner. If you do decide to include costumes or food in your book club, recognize that making those items may not be realistic for all members. Parents should discuss the scope of these projects in advance so nobody feels awkward or excluded.

KEEP IT SIMPLE. Lissa's adult book club always made book-themed dinners. She realized that every time she hosted, she spent the two weeks before stressing out about what she would serve. This made the group far less enjoyable for her. When she confessed her stress to the other members, most admitted they felt the same way. If you choose to have book-themed food or costumes at a book club meeting, keep it simple for the good of the group. No need to prepare a four-course meal or buy an expensive costume. A cupcake or wizard hat will do just as well! Costumes and food should enhance, not eclipse, the book discussions.

CRAFTS

Our group was the opposite of crafty. We couldn't get our kids to bust out glitter or glue guns for all the gold in Smaug's lair. But we did, for many, many years, get them to each do a drawing inspired by every book we read (see page 53). For our particular group of kids, we had to make it into a semi-competitive game to make it appealing: Show your book-themed drawing and see how many people can guess what it is. It's really fun now to look back on all the drawings they did over the years. The point is, even the

and then designed their own practical, girl-friendly armor.

When Meg's Tucson book club read *Umbrella Summer*, they created bookmarks out of popsicle sticks and brads (paper fasteners), which fanned out like umbrellas. They found instructions in the reader's guide for the book.

Pam's parent-daughters book club read a book that centered around birds, and the kids made peanut butter bird feeders. For holidays throughout the year, they tried to pick books with craft-friendly themes. One October they read a Halloween-themed book, then painted gourds.

least-crafty group can benefit from working a little artistic expression into their meeting. For more craft inspiration, we looked to our fellow parent-child book clubs.

Tasha is a children's librarian in Portland, Oregon. She started a book club for elementary-aged kids that focuses on graphic novels. Tasha's group puts aside twenty minutes out of every meeting for craft time, with activities always connected to the book. When her group read the graphic novel *Princeless*, they discussed the ridiculousness of women's armor in fantasy stories (which the book also critiques),

Crafts can be a great way for creative kids to get engaged with a book or for kids who aren't naturally creative to explore that side of themselves in the name of reading. You can often find craft and recipe ideas related to the book you're reading on the author's website, or in an online reader's guide, if the book has one available. Or, do a simple online search for *"book title* craft/recipe ideas" and you will find plenty of creative options to keep your group entertained.

MOVIE OUTINGS

Heading to the theater or curling up in someone's living room to watch a movie adaptation of the book we read was one of our group's favorite activities. Seeing movie adaptations gave us a different perspective on the story; allowed us to see someone else's interpretation of the characters, settings, and plot; and added an interesting layer to our book discussion. They were also great opportunities to bond with our group by spending time having fun together.

If we knew a movie adaptation of a book was coming out, we would intentionally pick that book to read the month before so we could plan a movie outing together. In those cases, we would go to a theater together and then a restaurant or coffee shop afterward to have our meeting, or watch it on TV at someone's home. We saw *How to Train Your Dragon* in the theater right when it first came out, and then went to Red Robin and had french fries and milkshakes, and talked about how the movie compared to the book, what they left out and why, and which was better. For the *Outsiders* movie, which was made in 1983, we rented it online and watched it at the host's house. When the movie was over we jumped right into our normal meeting. Movie outings do not have to be expensive—you can wait for the movie to come out on a streaming service, or go to a cheaper showing, such as a matinee or a weeknight, or see it at a second-run theater.

While our group almost always agreed that the book was better than the movie, we also agreed that watching movie adaptations together, whether at the theater or at home, was one of our favorite parts of book club.

AWESOME BOOK-TO-MOVIE (OR TV) ADAPTATIONS

It's great fun to read a book and then see the movie adaptation with your book club. An outing to the movie theater is easy enough that you could do it several times each year. Or you

and your child, or you and your book club, can just snuggle on the couch in your pj's. After watching, you can talk about how the book and movie were different, the same, and what you liked better about each one. There are tons of book-to-screen adaptions to choose from!

MIDDLE GRADE

- *Artemis Fowl* by Eoin Colfer
- *Because of Winn-Dixie* by Kate DiCamillo
- *Bridge to Terabithia* by Katherine Paterson
- *Charlie and the Chocolate Factory* by Roald Dahl (there is an eponymous 2005 movie, as well as a 1971 version, *Willy Wonka and the Chocolate Factory*)
- *Charlotte's Web* by E. B. White
- The Chronicles of Narnia series by C. S. Lewis
- *The City of Ember* by Jeanne DuPrau
- *Coraline* by Neil Gaimon
- Diary of a Wimpy Kid series by Jeff Kinney
- *Ella Enchanted* by Gail Carson Levine
- *Flora & Ulysses* by Kate DiCamillo **TV**
- *Freaky Friday* by Mary Rodgers (four great movies to choose from: 1976, 1995, 2003, 2018)
- *The Giver* by Lois Lowry
- *The Golden Compass* by Philip Pullman (there is also a TV adaptation, *His Dark Materials* **TV**)
- *The Great Gilly Hopkins* by Katherine Paterson
- Harry Potter series by J. K. Rowling
- *The Hobbit* and Lord of the Rings series by J. R. R. Tolkien (*The Hobbit* is a movie as well as a TV movie)
- *Holes* by Louis Sachar
- *Hoot* by Carl Hiaasen
- How to Train Your Dragon series by Cressida Cowell
- *Howl's Moving Castle* by Diana Wynne Jones
- *The Incredible Journey* by Sheila Burnford
- *The Invention of Hugo Cabret* by Brian Selznick (movie is *Hugo*)
- *James and the Giant Peach* by Roald Dahl

- *Love Double Dutch!* by Doreen Spicer-Dannelly (movie is *Jump In!*)

- *Mary Poppins* by P. L. Travers

- *Matilda* by Roald Dahl

- *My Side of the Mountain* by Jean Craighead George

- Percy Jackson and the Olympians series by Rick Riordan

- *The Princess Bride* by William Goldman (the movie is for ages 8+, the novel is for ages 14+)

- *The Princess Diaries* by Meg Cabot

- *The Secret Garden* by Frances Hodgson Burnett

- *A Series of Unfortunate Events* by Lemony Snicket (there is also a TV adaptation (TV))

- *The Spiderwick Chronicles* by Tony DiTerlizzi and Holly Black

- *Stuart Little* by E. B. White

- *The Tale of Despereaux* by Kate DiCamillo

- *Tuck Everlasting* by Natalie Babbitt

- *Where the Red Fern Grows* by Wilson Rawls

- *The Willoughbys* by Lois Lowry

- *The Wizard of Oz* by L. Frank Baum

- *Wonder* by R. J. Palacio

- *A Wrinkle in Time* by Madeleine L'Engle

YOUNG ADULT/ADULT CROSSOVER

- *1984* by George Orwell

- *The 5th Wave* by Rick Yancey

- *All the Bright Places* by Jennifer Niven

- *Before I Fall* by Lauren Oliver

- *The Book Thief* by Markus Zusak

- Divergent series by Veronica Roth

- *Emma* by Jane Austen (tons of movie adaptations to choose from—just pick an era!)

- *Ender's Game* by Orson Scott Card

- *Every Day* by David Levithan

- *Everything Everything* by Nicola Yoon

- *The Fault in Our Stars* by John Green

- *The Hate U Give* by Angie Thomas

- *The Hitchhiker's Guide to the Galaxy* by Douglas Adams

- The Hunger Games series by Suzanne Collins

- *I Am Number Four* by Pittacus Lore

- *If I Stay* by Gayle Forman

- *Jurassic Park* by Michael Crichton

- *The Knife of Never Letting Go* by Patrick Ness (movie is *Chaos Walking*)

- *Little Women* by Louisa May Alcott

- *Lord of the Flies* by William Golding

- *The Martian* by Andy Weir

- Maze Runner series by James Dashner

- *Me and Earl and the Dying Girl* by Jesse Andrews

- *The Miseducation of Cameron Post* by Emily Danforth

- *Miss Peregrine's Home for Peculiar Children* by Ransom Riggs

- *Naomi and Ely's No Kiss List* by Rachel Cohn and David Levithan

- *Nick and Norah's Infinite Playlist* by Rachel Cohn and David Levithan

- *The Outsiders* by S. E. Hinton

- *Paper Towns* by John Green

- *The Perks of Being a Wallflower* by Stephen Chbosky

- *Pride and Prejudice* by Jane Austen (another with many adaptations to pick from!)

- *Ready Player One* by Ernest Cline

- Scott Pilgrim graphic novel series by Bryan Lee O'Malley (movie is *Scott Pilgrim vs. the World*)

- *Simon vs. the Homo Sapiens Agenda* by Becky Albertalli (movie is *Love, Simon*)

- *The Sisterhood of the Traveling Pants* by Ann Brashares

- *Speak* by Laurie Halse Anderson

- *The Sun Is Also a Star* by Nicola Yoon

- *Ten* by Gretchen McNeil (watch the Agatha Christie movie *And Then There Were None*)

- To All the Boys series by Jenny Han

- *To Kill a Mockingbird* by Harper Lee

- Twilight series by Stephenie Meyer

- *Unbroken* by Laura Hillenbrand

- *Whip It* by Shauna Cross

PLAY OUTINGS

Just like going to movies, you can choose a book for your book club that has been adapted into a play. Check to see which plays are coming to your town and plan your reading list accordingly. Many books, comics, and graphic novels are also Broadway productions. Here are just a few.

- *Annie*
- *Dear Evan Hansen*
- *Fun Home*
- *Mary Poppins*
- *Matilda*
- *Peter Pan*
- *The Secret Garden*
- *Tuck Everlasting*
- *Wicked*

You can find even more playing at your local children's theater. You could also choose to read a play as your "book" choice and then act out a few scenes during your meeting, or try doing a small group performance from it.

AUTHOR EVENTS

Another fun book club activity is to go to an author signing for a book you've read together. Our group *adored* the Percy Jackson series and we read *The Lightning Thief* together as one of our earliest books. So when Rick Riordan came to town for a book signing at a local bookstore, we were all very excited to go. We made a full evening of it: We listened to Riordan speak, then waited in line with a thousand other fans in order to get our books signed and have a few seconds to chat with the legendary author. You can find out which authors are coming to your town by checking out these resources.

Author websites

If you have a particular author in mind, visit their website. If they have a new book coming out, they will usually have a tour schedule. If they don't have a new book, you can often sign up to be alerted when they'll next be in your area.

Your local library

Libraries also host author events. Check their website each month to see who is coming over the next few months. You could adjust your reading pick accordingly.

Bookstores

Many bookstores—especially children's bookstores—host author events. Most bookstores have event calendars you can visit online.

Make sure you and the kids come prepared with a few questions to ask the author. It makes the whole experience a lot more meaningful and memorable if someone in your group asks a question. And if you buy a copy of the author's newest book, stores will often let you bring their older books that you already have at home and get those signed as well.

AUTHOR VISITS TO YOUR BOOK CLUB

Believe it or not, some authors will actually come talk to your book club! Sometimes you have to purchase a certain number of books, but it's usually not that many. Shannon Watts, author and founder of Moms Demand Action, visited any book club that bought ten copies of her book, *Fight Like a Mother*. A local author might come to your meeting in person, while a not-local author could visit via Skype, Zoom, or another online platform. Check author websites to see if they do this sort of thing and how to contact them. (Author Kate Messner has a great website with a huge list of children's book authors willing do book club visits for free. See Resources on page 198.)

OTHER ACTIVITIES

There are a million fun activities you can do inspired by the books you read. You are limited only by your imagination. Here are a few more ideas to get you started.

Make a playlist

When we read *Ready Player One*—which is filled with references to 1980s movies, games, and music—the host created an '80s music playlist that played in the background through the entire meeting. The kids also played some retro video games during their Fun Time. Lots of authors (especially YA) create playlists that inspired their writing of a particular book. Check the author's website, then listen to their music and see what you think.

Do some journaling

When Meg's book club read *Walk Two Moons*, the host gave every kid a small notebook, each with a different quote from the book written in it. The kids read their quotes and wrote in their notebooks about what it meant to them.

Solve a mystery

When Kendra's book club read *The Westing Game*, the host created and organized a whodunit mystery game that the group had to solve together. This idea can work for any type of book, not just a mystery. You could also create your own Escape Room, where the kids have to solve the mystery to get out. The book *Holes* would work well for creating an Escape Room game, but you could use just about any mystery novel. See our list of mysteries and thrillers in chapter 9. Assign roles, write up clues, and let the sleuthing begin!

Hunt treasure

When Tasha's book club read *Marcy and the Riddle of the Sphinx*, she organized a book-themed treasure hunt for the kids. She gave each kid a list of items from the book that they had to go find. The kids could work on their own or in teams. The first one back with all the items was the winner. When our group read *Ready Player One*, the host organized a 1980s-themed treasure hunt. A hunt doesn't have to be difficult or complicated to be fun.

Invite a speaker

If the book you're reading focuses on a certain topic—say climate change, baseball, the Vietnam War—you could invite a speaker who is well-versed in the topic to come and talk to your group. Make sure your group is prepared with some good questions to ask your visitor—and extra snacks!

Volunteer

Sometimes a book you read may spark an interest that goes beyond book club. Issues of social justice, politics, and equity are common in books for teens and preteens. Reading a book could inspire your group to want to take action. Look for causes that relate to the book you read and use part of your meeting to write postcards, make calls, send texts, or put together care packages. Or you could go somewhere and volunteer. Here are some good options to consider.

- *March in a rally*

- *Walk or run in a fundraiser*

- *Work in a food bank or soup kitchen*

- *Help with a community or park cleanup*

- *Work at an animal shelter*

ACTIVITIES FOR OLDER KIDS

When your kids get older, they may not be as excited about doing crafts or games at book club (although our group has repeatedly refused to drop trivia since they love the thrill of a little competition). If you still want to mix it up a little at your meetings, you can try some activities that might appeal to the older crowd and still encourage them to do something a little different.

Do some writing

Many of the authors do unusual things in their writing, experimenting with form, narrator, or content. *The Book Thief* is narrated by Death. In *13 Reasons Why*, much of the novel is tape recordings. Kwame Alexander's Crossover novels are written entirely in free verse. It is interesting, especially when the kids are older, to spend time talking about what the author did and how. Our resident book editor,

Michelle, encouraged the kids to think like editors, to ask, "Which aspects of the book worked and which did not? Why?" You can turn this into a creative activity by inviting everyone to write a short piece in the author's style or from a similarly unique point of view. When we read *The Hate U Give*, for example, we talked about how the title is an acrostic—meaning the first letter of each title word spells out *THUG*. We discussed why the author put that "hidden word" in her title, then made our own acrostic poems.

Investigate the author

As our kids got older, we sometimes added an author research element to the book host duties—just a few minutes of web searching, nothing too difficult. Then the host would tell the group what they'd learned about the author and why they wrote the book. We encouraged all members to come to book club meeting with some "fun facts" about the author or the book. These details greatly enriched our understanding of the books and our discussions.

NOVEMBER IS NANOWRIMO MONTH!

Ann

One of the greatest unforeseen benefits of fostering a passion for reading in our kids has been fostering a love of writing as well. Over the years our kids got a lot of exposure to the different ways that writers choose to make their voices heard. The kids in our group are strong writers, and some are even pursuing their writing dreams in college.

While participating in book club, our family has also taken part in National Novel Writing Month (NaNoWriMo). Each November, we join hundreds of thousands of writers attempting to write full novels over one month, just for the fun of it. NaNoWriMo is a great organization (see Resources, page 198) to check out if you want to inspire your kids to express their own creative ideas on the page. If your book club likes to write, this would be a great activity to do together. Everyone writes their own novels in November, then you celebrate and read excerpts aloud at your December meeting.

A FINAL WORD

There are a ton of fun things you can add into your book club. It is really up to the adults in the group to decide how much energy to put into all the extra activities, and what will be fun and engaging for the kids. For us, the best route was to keep our meetings simple but to always have an easy game that the kids enjoyed. A discussion-only meeting would not have been popular and our group would not have lasted eleven years. In talking to other book clubs, we discovered that they, too, fondly recounted the different craft activities and the food themes they came up with. Games, food, and activities can definitely make a book club more fun, but figure out what works for you and what enhances the meetings. Don't let it take away from the most important part—reading together!

Chapter 6

Book Club Challenges

"How many others were walking around and not even knowing that someone far away cared for them? Imagine all that love floating in the air, waiting to land on someone's life!"

—from *Becoming Naomi León*
by Pam Muñoz Ryan

As you start your book club and get everything up and running, you are bound to hit some bumps along the way. Here are some common concerns and how to deal with them.

HOW CAN WE HELP YOUNGER KIDS ENJOY BOOK CLUB?

If your book club starts in early elementary school, the adults need to adjust the meeting and their expectations accordingly. Younger kids have shorter attention spans, so the discussion should be shorter and the playtime should be longer. Time of day is also important when scheduling the meeting. A first grader will have a harder time focusing right before dinner. Consider scheduling your meetings after school or on weekends,

between meals. We recommend book club snacks, but kids should not come to meetings needing breakfast, lunch, or dinner!

When your kids are young, meetings work best when structured around short, fun book-related activities. You might spend ten minutes sharing and discussing drawings; another fifteen minutes for a trivia game; then, take a snack break before continuing with the book ratings and discussion. Keep the book discussions short, ten to fifteen minutes. If a child struggles to come up with a discussion question, a parent can and should help them. Also, don't worry whether the kids' discussion questions are any good. "Which animal would you most like to be?" is a perfectly acceptable discussion question when they are little. The adults can pose a few deeper questions for the group to ponder.

HOW CAN WE HELP OLDER KIDS FIND TIME FOR BOOK CLUB?

When your kids are in elementary school they have lots of time to read for pleasure. As they get older, however, they will be much busier with school, sports, and other extracurricular activities. It may become harder for them to find time to read for fun. Being in a book club can help motivate older kids to keep reading because of the rewarding social aspect attached to it. If you are starting a book club with older kids, you might need to help them find a set time during the day or week when they can read for pleasure. That could be at bedtime, or on the weekends.

BOOK CLUB HELPS KEEP TEENS READING!

Michelle

As a children's book editor, I have a large collection of kids' books. Throughout elementary school, my kids were constantly knocking on my door asking to borrow books. When those same kids hit high school, however, the knocks stopped. Suddenly I had parents emailing me, "How do I get my teen to read again?!?" I noticed that teens who were not in a book club quit reading almost completely (especially the boys). Their parents were upset and baffled about what to do. I was and still am grateful that we had the book club during that time. Our teens' reading took a hit, but they never stopped and book club was a big part of that. Reading continued to be a fun, social activity. My son Ronan sent me this heart-warming text a few months into his college career: "I miss reading for fun. Will you send me some books?"

STRATEGIES FOR HIGH SCHOOL KIDS:

Dominic

Here are tactics that worked for me to make time for book club reading in high school.

- Schedule a time when you plan to read a book. You can even put it in your calendar.

- Don't try to read the entire book in one sitting. Spread it out over several readings.

- Use reading as a break from doing something more stressful (like calculus homework).

- If I just couldn't finish a book in time, I would skim the rest or read the SparkNotes summary so I could participate in the book discussion.

- Make sure the book club reading isn't stressing you out. It should be fun. If it is too much during a particularly busy month, take that month off.

Ronan

As we got busier in high school, here is how we adjusted our meetings to accommodate our schedules.

- We were lenient about attendance. We decided we needed three kids minimum to have a meeting. We got that low only a couple of times, and the meetings still went well.

- We were relaxed about finishing the book. Not everyone at our meetings always finished the book. Often a few people were still reading it, but they came and joined in the discussion and talked with friends.

- When things got extra busy (such as college application time), we spread our meetings further apart. Instead of every month, we met every six or eight weeks. Once the crunch was over, we went back to every four weeks.

- We used Doodle polls to schedule a meeting date when the most kids could be there.

WHAT IF THE KIDS ARE AT DIFFERENT READING LEVELS?

We all know that kids develop different skills at different rates. Some kids may be very comfortable reading chapter books but struggle to wait their turn to talk during book club meetings. Other kids may be fully capable of handling a group discussion but are still developing their independent reading skills. A book club can accommodate many different reading levels at the same time, as long as the kids have adult support.

To get started, all the kids don't have to be reading chapter books independently. Parents can read the book aloud with their child or get the audio version for them to listen to. In our early years, one boy's mom read the full books aloud to him. Another alternated reading chapters with their child. Two other kids listened to the audio versions of longer books. Your group can even discuss the different experiences of listening to a book versus reading it. How did the narrator sound? Did they do voices for different characters? What kind of voice did readers imagine?

Luci

When I was younger, I had a harder time following the plots of some books, especially if it was fantasy or sci-fi. My mom encouraged me to write a short summary after reading each chapter. This helped me break the book into manageable chunks so I could stick with it and not get totally lost. This also helped me have an informed opinion (or criticism) to share with the group during our book discussion.

Lissa

In sixth grade Noah struggled to understand *The Book Thief*. Its unusual structure—the narrator is "Death" telling the story of the other characters—made it difficult for him to follow the plot or connect with characters. To help, we read some of the challenging sections together and talked about what they meant. After we finished the book, we watched the movie together. It showed the plot in chronological order and made the characters more concrete. Thanks to these supports, Noah was able to fully participate in the discussion with the rest of the group.

WHAT IF THE BOOK I CHOOSE IS TERRIBLE AND EVERYONE HATES IT?

Do your research, read reviews, and make sure you are choosing books from a variety of genres. (And use our recommendations in part 2!) Beyond that, you can't control what other people think of a book. Usually some people like it and some don't. Sometimes *you* won't even like the book you chose. And that's OK. Don't put pressure on yourself or your kid to pick a book that everyone loves. It's hard to do. And to be honest, book discussions are way more interesting if some people like the book and others don't. It gives the group a lot more to talk about. It's even OK if *everyone* hates the book. Some of our best discussions were about books that all or most members strongly disliked. We really dug into what didn't work about the book and we look back on those stinkers fondly now. So don't worry about picking a bad book. If you do your book club right, there will be many, many more wonderful books to make up for it.

WHAT IF MY KID DOESN'T (OR I DON'T) FINISH THE BOOK?

Book clubs are a vehicle for reading and discussing books as a group. The expectation should be that kids and parents will finish the book by the time of the book club meeting. It is a good idea to lay out your expectations clearly in the first few meetings. Reading the whole book makes being at book club a lot more fun, and you avoid hearing spoilers!

But it's important to remember that book club is about more than the literary discussions. They are social events as well. We founded our book club with the stated expectation that everyone should try their best to read the book each month. And yet we've been pretty flexible with that rule. At any given meeting, there was usually one kid or parent who didn't have time to finish and we encouraged them to come anyway. Depending on how much they were able to read, they were usually able to participate in all the fun activities and even contribute to the discussion. Sometimes a person didn't finish a book because they didn't like it. When that happened, we would talk about why the book was not enjoyable and what could have made it more appealing to the people who disliked it. Everyone's perspective adds to the discussion.

That said, if you or your kid were unable to read *any* of the book, then it's best to stay home and leave the book discussion to those who read it. Also, if not reading the books becomes a pattern with one particular kid or parent, it's probably time for someone in the group to find out how they are feeling about book club. When someone stops reading the books on a regular basis, it often means they are ready to quit but just don't have the heart to tell their friends. An outside email or conversation can make this confession easier.

HOW STRICT SHOULD WE BE ABOUT ATTENDANCE?

The answer to this question depends on how old your kids are and how much help they might need from the grown-ups.

Younger kids need more guidance to stay focused and engaged during meetings, so parents should attend with their kids, prepared and ready to discuss. If a parent can't make it, they should contact another parent in the group to bring and support their child. If a child can't make it, that pair can stay home.

As the kids get older, they will require less and less parental help. By high school, they can most likely run their own book discussion easily and completely independent of parents.

In the later years, the parents in our group took a backseat at book club. We no longer had to read every book or attend every meeting. By and large, the kids ran things on their own. We parents always loved being in the book club, but eventually it became purely for pleasure.

WHAT IF MY KID LOSES INTEREST?

One challenge with a book club can be keeping your kid in it. This is definitely a hurdle that many book clubs will face as kids' interests, activities, and friendships change.

Over the years, we had several members who lost interest and quit the group. One member liked to read only nonfiction and mostly on one topic. Since he got to pick the book just once or twice a year, that meant he had to read a ton of books he didn't like. After a few years, he quit. Another member joined our club briefly, but after just a few meetings, he stopped reading the books. He explained that he didn't like reading books that other people chose and then having to discuss them. So, eventually, he stopped coming to the meetings.

Should the parents of these two kids have pushed them to stay in the book club when they didn't like it? We don't think so. The reality is that book club is a fun and rewarding experience for some and a chore for others. While parents should encourage their kids to try it and give it a chance for a few meetings, we don't recommend you push beyond that. If a kid is struggling with some particular aspect of book club, you can discuss it between the two of you and propose a solution to the rest of the group. For example, if your kid hates the game your group plays, they can sit that out or propose a different game they might like better. If your kid tried and hates reading a particular genre, they can skip it the next time that genre gets picked. But if they really just don't like or have time to be in a book club and there is no workaround, parents shouldn't force it. Pushing too hard could risk turning your kid off from reading entirely! While book clubs work for a wide variety of kids and adults, they are definitely not for everyone.

WHAT IF SOMEONE QUITS?

Sustaining a book club for many years means we saw several members come and go. Some moved away while others just decided to move on. Often when someone wants to leave, others in the book club try to talk them into staying. If there is an issue that can be addressed to keep that person in the group (as mentioned on page 89), then definitely try it and see if that fixes the problem. But usually talking someone into staying in the book club when they want to leave just delays the inevitable. Remember, a book club isn't the right fit for everyone.

When a family does leave, we recommend you find out why they left, to see if there are ways you might improve your book club moving forward. Then, move on. If you have enough members to continue, you don't need to do anything. A smaller group can mean more time for each person to share their thoughts. If the departure means you won't have enough people to keep going comfortably, then you'll need to invite in new members. See the next question for some ideas on how to do that.

HOW DO WE INVITE NEW MEMBERS?

There have been times during our book club journey when we needed to add new members after someone left, or we decided to increase the size of our group to add fresh ideas and voices. We did this as a group, meaning that during one of our book club meetings we talked as a group about different friends who might be interested in joining. Then we decided who would be the best fit and who would invite them. Sometimes the person said "no thanks," but other times we invited multiple new people and they all said "yes."

In our group, the first meeting a potential new member comes to is mostly a chance for them to get a sense of what the book club is all about. If they like it after that first meeting, then they commit to it for the long haul. It's really important to make new members feel welcome. If your book club has been together for a long time, there are bound to be inside jokes and history that the new members won't get. Make sure they understand the games and activities of your group and invite them to participate if they seem shy. Perhaps let them pick the next book, so they feel involved. Make sure they have fun and feel welcome by all members.

HOW DO WE DISCUSS SENSITIVE TOPICS?

Over the years our reading list became more and more mature, and yours surely will too. We went from innocent books like the Hardy Boys series, *Rascal,* and *Tales of a Fourth Grade Nothing*, to books with some very difficult topics, like *The Hate U Give* (racism and police violence), *Tweak* (drug addiction and teen prostitution), and *The Perks of Being a Wallflower* (mental illness and child sexual abuse). While it is very rewarding to discuss books with more challenging topics, it can be difficult to decide when kids and parents are ready for them.

If you are choosing the book and discover that it has some sensitive material in it, you should read the reviews carefully. You might even decide to pre-read the book or at least those scenes, to see for yourself how you feel about your child and group reading it. Once you know what's in the book, communicate that to the rest of the group. You can share reviews or let parents know which sections of the book they can pre-read. If enough members want to read the book, then by all means carry on with your meeting. However, if most members don't think the group is ready yet, you should probably put the book on hold for a while. Of course, you and your child can still read it.

In our group, we did not shy away from books with more difficult themes, but we had an open conversation about the book beforehand, and then we let each person decide if they were ready for a particular topic. If not, they could bow out of reading that book and skip the meeting.

If you do move forward with reading a book that tackles challenging issues, you need to prepare more thoughtfully for the discussion. Before the group discussion, the host or another parent should talk to the group about the importance of discussing the book's topics in a thoughtful, respectful manner. It's more important than ever to listen, not interrupt, and be open to other members' thoughts and opinions. The entire group should work hard to discuss these topics in appropriate and respectful ways.

Over the years, there have been a few books that led to a serious debate over whether or not we should read them as a group. *The Hunger Games* and *Unwind* were two books that we questioned for their violent and disturbing content. Ultimately, our group decided to read them, but a few members opted to not participate those months. *13 Reasons Why* was the one book our group considered reading but decided not to. We read the reviews and decided as a group that we were worried that it romanticized suicide. Many kids in the group did read the book eventually, but we didn't do it together.

Both the kids and parents need to make judgment calls about when it is

appropriate to read and discuss books with difficult and sensitive topics. Do your research and make a decision that feels right to you. Not everyone will be ready to discuss these topics at the same time, and that's OK. But we encourage you to include these books in your reading list. They make for wonderful, eye-opening discussions—possibly the best you will have.

WHY READING AND DISCUSSING CHALLENGING BOOKS IS GOOD FOR KIDS:

Noah

One of the most difficult books we read was *Tweak: Growing Up on Methamphetamines* by Nic Sheff. It's a memoir of a young man whose life is spiraling out of control because of his growing drug addiction. The book was disturbing to read, but also fascinating since most of us had not been exposed to such a coherent firsthand account of drug addiction. It was frustrating to watch this teenager make one bad decision after another, and some passages described vivid and uncensored scenes of addiction.

We discussed ahead of time whether our group was ready for the book and a few people decided to skip it. While the kids who read it had no problem with the content, our parents were a different story. The book contained some of the most mature content we had read in book club, and it's a memoir about a real teenager's life. Some parents were uneasy about us reading it, unsure how we would process and react to these topics.

To their surprise, we had one of the best book discussions ever. We kids were puzzled by the many bad decisions the character made, so we discussed the psychology of drug addiction. We discussed the character's life, and how family problems can both cause and be caused by drug addiction. We also talked about how hard it is to get clean after being addicted to drugs and how it could happen to anyone (the main character was white and from a wealthy family).

While lighthearted books are fun to read, it is the more difficult books about real-life issues that have inspired our group's best discussions. Diving into these topics when kids are ready for them may be difficult and uncomfortable for both the parents and kids but can really add to the book club experience.

WHAT IF SOMEONE TALKS TOO MUCH?

Sometimes a kid or parent may talk more than others in a discussion because they read the book more carefully or they really enjoyed it. This is less than ideal, especially if it's an adult doing all the talking. You want to make sure everyone in your group gets a chance to talk, express their opinions, and feel heard. Here are some ways to make sure everyone gets an equal opportunity.

- *Set a time limit for talking. You can use an hourglass or a watch timer.*

- *Assign someone to call on people who haven't contributed yet.*

- Pass out two coins to each person. Each time they speak, they put a coin in a bowl. When their coins are gone, they have to wait until the next round of questions to speak again.

- When a person finishes, they choose the next person to speak, until everyone has had a turn.

WHAT IF SOMEONE DOESN'T TALK ENOUGH?

There can be a lot of reasons why someone doesn't want to speak in a book club discussion. Maybe it's shyness; maybe it's lack of preparation; maybe it's feeling on the outs socially with the group; maybe it's disinterest in the topic. But there are a number of relatively easy techniques to help a kid who is feeling worried about participating in the group for any reason.

Share a question

Encourage the kid to prepare a discussion question. Coming up with a question that reflects their interests will make it easier to find a way into the conversation.

Read a passage

Ask the kid to find a few lines or a moment in the story that they thought was interesting or funny. During the discussion, they can share that passage and ask if the other kids found it interesting too.

Read a book review

Reading a review of the book can help kids discover what others found interesting and help them come up with a topic for discussion. They can even read the review and ask if other kids agree or disagree with the reviewer's opinion.

Write a comment

The act of writing a few sentences about the book can help a lot in being comfortable speaking up in the group. If a kid spends just a few minutes preparing a comment to read to the group, it helps them feel more confident and able to articulate their thoughts.

Assign someone to be "the inviter"

Give one adult the job of keeping track of the conversation and inviting reluctant speakers to participate. In our group it's pretty simple. Kristin usually keeps track and will say, "We haven't heard from Noah yet. Noah, what do you think about that?" If every kid knows they will be given a chance to talk, they don't have to worry about jumping in and can just wait until it's their turn.

Some people have a harder time sharing their opinions in a group than others. Some people, especially kids, fear they'll say something "stupid" or be laughed at. It's the adults' job to make book club a safe place for everyone to share their thoughts. You can help reluctant kids gain confidence by inviting them in. The more they practice, the more comfortable they'll become.

TIPS ON GETTING COMFORTABLE WITH TALKING:

Noah

Writing my discussion questions out helped me feel more prepared. It forced me to think about the book's plot, characters, and themes. When I asked my question, I had some control over the discussion and could talk about topics I'm interested in. I felt a sense of pride when I came up with a topic that got a good discussion going and inspired different opinions. That confidence is critical for those who feel less comfortable talking during book discussions.

The book ratings are also a good tool to help people feel comfortable speaking up. Coming up with a rating is easy, but it gives everyone a chance to talk about what they thought of the book and listen to everyone else's opinions. It doesn't take much thought, but it gets the conversation going. If someone gave the book a rating of two, we can talk about why they hated it. If they gave it a nine, we can talk about what they thought was so great. Some excellent conversations happened when our ratings spanned the scale.

WHAT IF A DISCUSSION OFFENDS SOMEONE, OR WORSE, CAUSES SOMEONE HARM?

If you read a variety of books, you are bound to encounter some tough topics or sensitive issues, which may make some people in your group uncomfortable or cause them real harm. As your kids grow and mature, they will go through a maelstrom of changes that may include developments in gender or sexual identity, increased awareness of racial politics and how their racial or ethnic identity is depicted in a book, or a growing sense of socioeconomic inequality and how privilege might shape the lives of some of the characters or even fellow members of the book club. In an ideal world, it would be possible for the person who has been harmed to speak up. But in the real world, it is really hard to speak up when someone has just hurt you.

When you are first forming your book club, it is really helpful to talk explicitly about how the group will deal with hurt feelings. By talking about it outside of the context of a specific situation, it is a lot easier to avoid landmines when they arise. It also avoids calling out kids whose

identity might be represented, or misrepresented, in a particular book. In other words, you should all talk about what you will do if you encounter racism or other forms of discrimination in the books you read, rather than waiting until you read a book with racist or racially charged content.

There are several ways to approach this. When the kids are young, this might take the form of a quick discussion about how the members should think about others' feelings when they speak. It could also include a few rules for how to talk about difficult topics. Sometimes older books use words that we would now consider racist or hurtful. It helps for kids to talk about the words we use when talking about identities that are not our own, and how to be respectful of the changing vocabulary around identity.

Your book club should decide what members should do if they feel offended or hurt. This might be something like saying "ouch" to let the group know that someone said something that hurt their feelings. It could be letting the host know during a break that someone said something that was insensitive. Whatever the group decides, it really helps for each person in the group to know that other members care about them and don't want to hurt their feelings, and that there's a safe way to talk about those feelings. Conversations about why something is hurtful or offensive to someone else can be powerful lessons for everyone involved.

HOW DO WE NAVIGATE CHANGING FRIENDSHIPS?

Our book club was founded by a group of friends. The kids were in the same kindergarten class and were already close (as close as kindergarteners can get, anyway), and we parents were getting to know each other. It was easy to motivate the kids to come and participate in book club because it was also a playdate! The kids' friendship lasted all the way through elementary school, which made book club really enjoyable for everyone.

In middle school things started to change. Dominic transferred to a different school and the rest of the group branched out into new friend groups. Some members still hung out together at school, but others had new friend groups that didn't include any book club members. There was some overlap, but it wasn't the same as before.

When starting a parent-child book club, it's inevitable that your kids will have some shifting of friends and social groups as the years go on. This can be difficult to navigate. It may become harder to motivate your kids to continue with book club if they aren't as close with the kids. It can also be awkward for them to discuss sensitive book topics with kids they

no longer consider close friends. This awkwardness seemed most pronounced in middle school. If you can get the group through those years, it seems to be easier in high school. Here are a few tips for persevering through the awkward times.

- *Try to make sure every kid member has at least one friend in the group. That may mean letting a member invite someone new into the group whom they feel close to.*

- *Have conversations about how to talk respectfully about sensitive issues and about how to listen to the thoughts and opinions of everyone in the group.*

- *If conflicts come up at a book club meeting, or behind the scenes, a parent should get involved and talk with the kids.*

Some book clubs may experience a more serious issue than the natural shifting of friend groups. There could be hurt feelings or an actual conflict between members who are not getting along. If this happens, adults should step in to find out what's going on and mediate the conflict. It's better to have this conversation outside of the book club meeting. It's also possible that the book club can help mend fences. Sometimes talking about a

fictional character's friendship issues can help kids find solutions to their own problems. That's what reading is all about.

HOW CAN WE CREATE AN INCLUSIVE ATMOSPHERE FOR OUR BOOK CLUB?

Any kind of social gathering in elementary, middle, and high school can create feelings of exclusion for kids and their parents. Book club is no exception. Some kids might come to book club meetings worried about whether they fit into the group, nervous about whether they are reading as well as the others, or petrified about embarrassing themselves in front of their peers when they speak. Some parents might feel anxious about whether they fit in with the other parents, concerned to see that their kid isn't as popular as the other kids, or panicked at the prospect of needing to try to analyze kids' books. Some book club participants may also be struggling with financial worries, health concerns, or family difficulties that they don't want to share with the group. Keeping these things in mind when hosting a book club meeting helps create an inclusive environment that recognizes that everyone brings both valuable perspectives as well as hidden stresses to group events.

When hosting a meeting, the time before the book discussion starts is a wonderful opportunity to get to know both the kids and parents better and begin to help everyone feel like the important member of the group they are. Explicitly avoiding discussion topics that might make one of the kids or parents feel left out (for example, vacation plans, gatherings where not everyone is invited, or volunteer opportunities at school when some parents work full-time) can go a long way to help everyone feel included. Show genuine interest in new members and make a concerted effort to avoid breaking off into smaller groups with established friends.

The best part about book club, of course, is that you all *always* have one thing in common: the book! As long as you are sensitive to the fact that there are varying degrees of comfort participating in the discussion (for both kids and adults), the discussion of the book is the best place to create inclusivity. It feels wonderful when someone truly cares what you think and asks for your opinion. It's amazing when someone responds to a comment you make and builds on what you just said.

Luci

In our book club it has been really helpful that we used to be super close and are still at least casual friends with one another. We have a long history, and it's fun to look back together at the things we did when we were little. Now that we are in college, we see each other a lot less. Part of our book club meetings are spent catching up. We talk about how school and sports are going, what classes we're taking, and other things happening in our lives. We all get along very well, which means it's still fun to go to meetings.

These are all ways to build an inclusive community and show how you truly value what each person says. The more the group practices listening to one another, responding to one another, and affirming the value of each person's contribution, the more inclusive it will feel.

A FINAL WORD

While there are plenty of potential challenges when starting a book club with your kids, we believe it's easier than most people think. In all our years together, we had very few problems, and the problems we had were fairly easy to navigate. We wish you all smooth and easy sailing with forming your book club. We believe that even if you have some setbacks, what you will gain will be more than worth it.

Part 2

CHOOSIN

YOU

BOOKS

Chapter 7

How to Pick
Great Books

"They're just wildflowers, doing their thing, and they're beautiful. Be like them, sweet pea. Just be you and be happy."

—from *This Time Will Be Different*
by Misa Sugiura

Now that you've decided on the members of your book club, how to set it up, and how to structure meetings, it's time to choose your first book! This chapter gives you guidance on how to choose great books that will spark meaningful discussions and keep your group thriving for years to come.

The rest of the chapters in part 2 are full of book recommendations to help you with your search. Chapter 8 lists the one hundred books our group read, with descriptions of the books, plus what our members thought of them. Chapter 9 has one hundred more books that we love, chapter 10 has one hundred amazing books with diverse protagonists, and chapter 11 has one hundred great graphic novels. That's a lot of books to choose from! You should be able to find any type of book you might be looking for.

CHOOSING THE RIGHT AGE LEVEL

As kids grow, their maturity and taste in books also grows. You can't keep reading middle grade books when your kids are in high school, as much as you might want to. The kids will lose interest and quit. But moving up to the next age category can be a difficult transition. Some kids may be ready for older, more challenging books before their friends are ready. Some kids may be ready for that transition before their parents are ready.

In our book club, this was an issue we wrestled with at each transition: from chapter books to middle grade to young adult novels. We progressed through these age levels with much group discussion and some mistakes. There were some books we read too early and some books we read later than we needed to. While there is no hard, set answer for when you should begin reading each age category, it does help to know what those categories are.

Chapter books

It's pretty hard to start a parent-child book club before your kids can read independently, so the first age category we're including are "chapter books" (or "chapter books for beginning readers"). These are shorter, simpler stories, aimed at kids ages six to ten, and usually under one hundred pages. These books are best for kids who have moved beyond picture books and leveled readers, who know how to read, but aren't great at it yet. Some popular chapter book series are Alvin Ho, the Clubhouse Mysteries, Meet Yasmin!, Mercy Watson, and Zapato Power.

Middle grade

These are for kids ages eight to twelve. The books are longer, but usually not as long as young adult books. Even though middle grade books aren't aimed at an adult audience, that doesn't mean they aren't good. One of our favorite books we ever read in book club was *Wonder*, a middle grade novel. Middle grade books deal with topics more appropriate for elementary-aged kids, like school, friendship, pets, siblings, family issues, and puberty. Romantic situations are usually limited to hand holding and kissing, if there are any at all. When there is violence, it's less graphic and gory than young adult books. Popular middle grade novels include *Because of Winn-Dixie*; *Bud, Not Buddy*; *Charlotte's Web*; *Ella Enchanted*; *Esperanza Rising*; *Ghost*; *Holes*; and *Wonder*.

Young adult

Young adult (YA) books are aimed at kids in middle and high school, ages twelve and up (or less frequently, fourteen and up). YA books are often as long as adult books and full of topics that are just as meaty, but with teen protagonists and themes that will resonate with younger readers. Be warned: YA books can cover very difficult topics and themes. Violence, suicide, alcohol, drugs, and sex are not uncommon. Adults are not always the good guys and endings aren't always happy. Real-world problems are presented, and not in a sugar-coated way.

The move up to YA books can be challenging for a parent-child book club. Some kids may not be ready for YA content and some parents definitely may not be. When you first begin reading YA books, take even more care to read reviews of the books, or even pre-read them if that will help you be more confident your group is ready.

A book's intended audience, or age range, is usually listed in the publisher information. You can also find this information on the author's website. At libraries or bookstores, books are shelved in separate sections for each of these age categories. Middle grade books are labeled as such, as are young adult (which are also sometimes called "teen").

If your book club lasts as long as ours did, you'll probably read books in all of these categories (and maybe some adult books as well). Deciding when it's appropriate to move up to the next level can be challenging depending on the content or difficulty of the book. It's important to be flexible and decide on a case-by-case basis. No one rule works for every book.

The Hunger Games and *The Fault in Our Stars*. Many of our kids were perfectly capable of reading these books, but they were written for kids ages fourteen and up and had content that was definitely not intended for younger kids.

SHOULD WE READ ABOVE AGE LEVEL?

This is a question our group wrestled with primarily when our kids were between the ages of ten and fourteen. Around fifth grade our kids started asking to read popular YA books like

Michelle

I hear kids and parents brag about how young a child was when they read a book that was written for much older readers. It usually makes me sad. Not because I think that child was scarred by the sex, drugs, or swearing they might have read in the book, but because they will most likely have missed something important the author was trying to convey. If the author wrote the book for an older audience, there was a reason. The author wanted to share an experience or a theme with readers in a particular age range for whom it would resonate most.

For example, *The Fault in Our Stars* is a love story. The sex scene is pretty tame, so it's not completely inappropriate for younger readers. But ten-year-olds are generally not falling in love and having sex for the first time. While it might be titillating, the experiences in the book won't mean nearly as much to a ten-year-old as they will to that same kid when they are older. Sadly, if a kid reads a book too young, they usually won't read it again. They may not have liked it and they certainly will miss out on the deeper connection they could have with the story when they are going through the same experiences as the characters in it. This is the reason I encourage parents and kids to wait until their kids are in the target age range—so they get a chance to connect with the characters and themes when they will have the most meaning.

In our book club, we worked hard to find books that were challenging for our strong readers but had content and themes that were appropriate for their age. That is, books for middle grade kids that are more challenging to read (length, vocabulary, complex plots and characters), but not too advanced in terms of themes. For example, *Harry Potter and the Sorcerer's Stone* was the first book we read when the kids were in first grade. Even though the book is aimed at a slightly older audience (ages 8+) than first graders, the kids loved reading it, and we were able to have a good discussion because its themes weren't too far over their heads (Be aware: Later books in the series *are* aimed at older readers and do have more mature themes.)

Occasionally, we messed up and picked a book that was too old for our kids. The two that come to mind are *A Wrinkle in Time* and *The Book Thief*. Our kids were able to read both books but didn't enjoy them as much as they might have had they been older. In both cases, the parents had to help with the discussion a lot more than we normally would. There have been other times, however, when our kids did comprehend "older" themes earlier than we expected. Deciding whether the kids in your group are ready for a book aimed at older readers is a personal decision. We can tell you that from our own experience, it can work well or it can flop. But it's not the end of the world—there's always the next book to look forward to.

CHOOSING A GENRE

The key to keeping your book club fun and interesting over the years is book *variety*. If you set your sights on varying the kinds of books you read each month, it's hard to go wrong. While there might be some adult book clubs that can focus on one genre (like all sci-fi or all memoir), the beauty of doing a book club with kids who are growing and changing is that it can expose them to all different kinds of books. It will help them discover and fall in love with books and genres they never would have tried otherwise. And it will help you too!

Once you decide which age level your child and group is ready for, you can then turn to the genre. Do your best to vary the literary genres you read over the course of the year. Even if all the kids in your group prefer one genre, it is still good to expose them to different kinds of writing and stories. Here are the main genres to sample from.

○ **Realistic Fiction:** *Stories that are made up but could happen in real life. Stories that are filled with action, adventure, or humor would be classified as realistic fiction first.*

○ **Historical Fiction:** *Stories that are made up but based on true events in history.*

○ **Fantasy:** *Stories that are made up and include elements that could not happen in real life, such as magic, supernatural elements, or talking animals.*

○ **Science Fiction:** *Stories that tie in with science and technology, often set in the future. Dystopian novels are usually science fiction or fantasy.*

○ **Mystery:** *Stories that involve a secret or crime that needs to be solved.*

○ **Graphic Novel:** *A story told in comic strip format (with sequential art, usually in panels). Graphic novels can also fall in any of these other genres. For example, a graphic novel can be sci-fi, realistic fiction, memoir, or nonfiction.*

○ **Nonfiction:** *Books that present factual information about a particular topic like sports, animals, or historical events.*

○ **Biography, Autobiography, or Memoir:** *An account of someone's life written by the person (autobiography or memoir) or by someone else (biography).*

CHOOSING BOOKS WITH DISCUSSION POTENTIAL

A good book club pick should allow you to discuss more than just the plot of the book. A great choice will allow you and your kids to think about questions and perspectives that you hadn't thought about before. All genres of kids' books can foster these kinds of questions, so be open to all the options out there. You can't predict how a book will be received by the group, of course, but you can ensure a good discussion. Consider some of the following questions to help you decide if it will produce a good discussion.

○ *Does the book touch on an important and timely social issue?*

○ *Does the story take place in an alternate world that challenges how we see our world?*

○ *Is the book written in an unusual form, and does that form help express its themes?*

○ *Do the story's characters have different life experiences than the kids in your group?*

○ *Does the story contain dilemmas or choices that your group can debate for themselves?*

○ *Does the book have any experimental elements? For example, a unique narrator, time jumps, multiple points of view, unusual design or typography?*

Ronan

It's important to remember that you don't *always* have to choose a book that is super deep. Sometimes it's nice to read a book just for fun. If it's well written, even a "pleasure read" can make for a good book club discussion. There will be conflict and character dilemmas you can talk about. It's good to have a mix of books that are fun to read and books that are more intellectual. The best books (for book clubs or not) are both.

BATTLE OF THE BOOKS—ANOTHER PLACE TO FIND GREAT BOOKS:

Owen

Battle of the Books is a national reading contest for kids. For five years, the kids in our book club competed in our state's Battle of the Books tournament. The contest was a great chance for us to test our trivia skills, honed over years of fierce competition within our book club. But it also helped us expand the variety of books we read. Each year, the sixteen books chosen spanned every genre and topic, from a punk graphic novel reimagining of Rapunzel to a nonfiction biography of The Beatles. I read many books for Battle of the Books that I would never have picked up on my own, and many of them I greatly enjoyed. The contest was a fun, fascinating experience for our group, but more importantly, it helped us see the value of reading a wide variety of books. Your state's annual Battle of the Books reading list is a great place to look for good books. It will even have local authors to choose from.

Photo in the paper after the kids won the regional Oregon Battle of the Books competition.

CHOOSING "CLASSICS"— TO READ OR NOT TO READ, THAT IS THE QUESTION!

When organizing a book club for kids and parents, it might be tempting to read a lot of classic works of literature while you have a chance to choose which books your kids will read. Let us assure you that your book club will suffer a swift demise if the kids feel like they are only reading books that feel like homework. But that doesn't mean you shouldn't bring in the occasional classic to expose them to times and places from long ago.

Contemporary books are exciting to read, can engage your group with current issues, and feel very relevant to the kids. Contemporary books are also written by more diverse authors who can expose your child to characters, thoughts, and places they have never experienced. There are a wealth of viewpoints to choose from on the modern bookshelf. But it's also worth it to sprinkle in a few older works on your list. When your kids get to high school and college, they will benefit from having read some books that feel old to them and require more work to understand.

You can also have incredibly rich discussions with your kids about how worldviews, language, and word meanings have changed over the years. When you read older books, it's a great opportunity to talk with your group about why certain books became "classics" and others didn't. You can talk about whose viewpoints are *not* represented in these books. You can help them understand how certain books present outdated, inaccurate, or harmful views of certain cultures, races, or socioeconomic groups. While having those conversations might be difficult, they give your kids a sense of history and the struggles that different groups have faced.

Most important, reading older works will help your child recognize the value of looking beyond the narrow limits of the current moment. It's in our nature to think that we've got it all figured out and people in the past were just wrong. Reading books written in earlier times shows us that writers have been asking the same questions for hundreds or even thousands of years. Spending some time trying to understand their answers to those questions and seeing what they got right or overlooked can help us question whether our own answers might be missing something. These books can humble us and help us recognize how much we still do not know.

Don't forget that the classics, in their time, were often revolutionary and established new literary trends that inspired a host of authors following in their footsteps. *The Catcher in the Rye* is considered by many to be the first YA novel, and its tale of teenage alienation was radical at the time. Twenty years later, S. E. Hinton continued to explore those themes in *The Outsiders*. Today we see a ton of books written about teenagers growing up in a world in which they feel they don't belong. In our book club, we read *The Perks of Being a Wallflower*, *The Fault in Our Stars*, and *All the Bright Places*, all of which draw on those same themes. Reading some classics allows you to discuss and compare books from different eras that touch on universal themes.

HARMFUL OR OFFENSIVE LANGUAGE:

Ann

Some "classics" contain language you don't want your kid using in book club or with other kids. This might include racial slurs or problematic language around gender, sexuality, class, or physical disability. Be aware that this kind of language risks causing real harm to members of your group and you will want to proceed with great caution. If anyone is going to feel singled out or targeted by reading or discussing a book with hurtful language, just skip it.

That said, if you do read a book with offensive language, it can be a good opportunity to have a discussion with your kid and the rest of the book club members about how language and word choice can really hurt people. In the context of a story, kids can see how language can be very harmful in concrete but not personalized ways. Learning the history of how certain terms have been used can help kids understand why members of a particular group might be harmed by those words and have strong preferences for one term over another.

CHOOSING BOOKS BY DIVERSE AUTHORS

No matter which communities your book club members belong to, it's critical that you read diverse books by diverse authors. As Gene Luen Yang, former National Ambassador for Young People's Literature, put it: "Stories have two different purposes. Stories act as a window into somebody else's life, and they act as a mirror into your own." When choosing books to read, you should look for both: books that are mirrors, with characters who look like your kids and/or share their experiences; and books that are windows into someone else's experience, by authors who have lived that experience. Research shows that reading books by and about people who are different from you is one of the best ways to understand another point of view and to develop empathy.

After a long and shameful lack of children's books written by and about marginalized groups (including Black, Indigenous, and people of color [BIPOC]; lesbian, gay, bisexual, transgender, and queer-identified people [LGBTQ+]; and people with disabilities), movements like We Need Diverse Books have helped push open the publishing gates, and a flood of talent is finally pouring in. It is now much easier to find diverse writers and books. Although there is still a long, long way to go to reach equitable representation in children's literature, there are so many amazing books to choose from, and there is zero excuse not to read books by diverse authors. All of our lists of recommended books feature books by diverse authors. And chapter 10 has recommendations for books with diverse protagonists that you can (and should) explore more deeply.

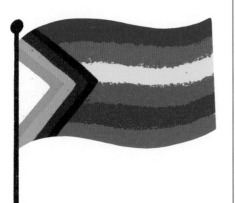

GENDER STEREOTYPES IN BOOKS:

Owen

It is important to pick a balance of books with straight, queer, male, female, nonbinary, cisgender, and transgender characters. In our book club we have always been sure to include plenty of books with female leads. Some of our favorite books have strong female protagonists: *The Hunger Games*, the Amulet graphic novel series, *The Hate U Give*, and *Daughter of Smoke & Bone*. When we read *Every Day*, the story of an entity that changed bodies every day, it led to thoughtful and insightful conversations about whether gender was a defining factor of love. The books you choose can challenge commonly held beliefs and will help your kids see that people should not be confined to narrow roles or expectations.

Luci

At a very young age, kids are exposed to lots of gender stereotypes in our world. It happens with toys, movies, sports, and yes, books too. Girls are often expected to read "girl books" about princesses, fairies, and romance. Boys are expected to like "boy books" about adventure and sports. This kind of gender simplification should be avoided in your book club. Labeling books as being for girls or boys, or encouraging kids to only read books that align with their gender will unnecessarily limit the options for kids who want to read books outside those stereotypes. When our group began, I was the only girl with four boys. Over the years we have added more girl members, as well as members who identify as BIPOC. With more diverse members, the books we read have gotten more diverse as well. I like that people in our book club are open to reading any book. We have never labeled the books we read as "girl" or "boy" books.

READING REVIEWS

Once you find a book you are interested in, read the reviews. This is the best place to find out what age it's appropriate for, possible discussion topics, and potential areas of concern. Here are some good places to look for reviews.

Common Sense Media

This group reviews children's books and other content (movies, video games, and so on) for parents. They also highlight and explain potential areas of concern, like language, violence, drug and alcohol use, etc. Our group is divided on the usefulness of this website. The parents find their rating system and reviews quite helpful, while many of the kids feel their age ratings are too one-size-fits-all. See the sidebar on page 120 for the pros and cons of using Common Sense Media to help you choose books. Also, Common Sense does not review all books, so you may not find a review of the book you are interested in. (See Resources, page 198.)

Amazon Editorial Reviews

If you type in a book title on Amazon, down below the book description and ads for other books, you will find a section called "Editorial Reviews." There you will be able to see if the book has won any awards, earned starred reviews, and/or been evaluated by reputable children's book reviewers, such as *Booklist, Kirkus, Publishers Weekly,* and *School Library Journal.*

Amazon has another helpful section titled "Customers who viewed this item also viewed." This is a great place to search for similar books. If your group loved *Ghost* by Jason Reynolds, you can look it up on Amazon, then search the "Customers who viewed this item" bar and see similar titles, usually for the same age range. Be aware: Amazon sometimes puts this bar up top, under the book description. But sometimes they put it at the bottom, nearly at the end of the page. "Books you may like" and "Products related to this item" are paid advertising. Not the same!

Author and Publisher Websites

The author and publisher websites usually have the book's age range, awards, and reviews.

Bookstores

Many bookstores will have a wealth of ideas for you. If you are lucky and have a children's bookstore in town, they are great places to ask for recommendations. They know their books! If you're in a regular bookstore, ask to talk to someone who works in the kid's section.

Teachers and Librarians

Teachers and librarians (especially children's librarians) are fabulous resources for book recommendations and are usually familiar with how appropriate certain books are for different ages. They have read tons of books, pay attention to awards and reviews, and know which books are popular with kids.

Friends

Friends of the kids or parents in your group can be another great resource for book recommendations. Kids are also likely to want to read what their friends are reading.

COMMON SENSE PROS AND CONS:

Kristin

When looking books up on Common Sense Media, I look at the age they recommend it for, but I take that with a grain of salt. I know what concerns me in regards to my child. They have a section called "A Lot or a Little? The parents' guide to what's in the book" that describes what you might find in a book that could be concerning (violence, sex, drinking and drugs, language). I can use those descriptions to decide if it's something my child is ready for. My concerns about what my child reads have changed as she's gotten older. Swear words might have been a concern when she was seven, but not when she was seventeen. Characters drinking might be OK for my fourteen-year old, depending on how it's depicted. Common Sense Media describes these areas so you, the parent, can decide.

Sometimes a Common Sense review would make me realize that I actually needed to read the book for myself. After reading their review of *The Hunger Games*, I decided to pre-read it. I realized it wasn't the violence that bothered me, but that the concepts were too mature for my daughter

when she wanted to read it. Overall, Common Sense has been a great tool for deciding if the kids are ready to read a book, or if we should wait a bit.

Dominic

Growing up, Common Sense annoyed me with their seemingly arbitrary age ratings. When I wanted to read a book, my parents would look at the recommended age, and that pretty much determined if I could read it or not. Although it was convenient for my parents, those age ratings are one person's opinion and don't take into account all of the relevant factors.

Their descriptions of specific violence, language, or sexual themes are helpful, but by distilling all that information into one number (recommended age), they make it difficult for parents to come to a different conclusion. What they *should* do is to provide only a review and objective descriptions of potentially troublesome content and then let parents make the subjective decision about whether to allow their kid to read it. As is, I would encourage parents to ignore their age ratings and decide from the full reviews instead.

A FINAL NOTE

There are a lot of factors to keep in mind when choosing a book for your book club. You want to make sure the kids have a hand in the choosing, but that the books represent a good mix of genres and perspectives, and that they are both fun and thought-provoking. But don't worry *too* much about it. It's important to think about all these things, but not every book will be a winner. You and others in your group are bound to choose some books that people don't like. That's part of the fun! Remember that there's always next month. And the month after that. If you keep your book club enjoyable and your book choices diverse, you will read so many amazing books. That's what it's all about.

Chapter 8

One Hundred Books We Read in Book Club

"I fell in love the way

you fall asleep: slowly,

and then all at once."

—from *The Fault in Our Stars*

by John Greene

This is the list of all the books we read during our eleven years of book club. They are listed chronologically, so the list starts with middle grade books and moves into young adult books (for the most part) as our kids got older. The first book our group read was a middle grade novel, because that's what our kids were reading when we began. That does not mean you can't start a group reading chapter books first—you certainly can! Also, nearly all of these books (and books in the lists that follow) have audiobook versions, if that is something you need or want.

Not all of these are great books because not every book we chose was a winner. But there are a lot of amazing books in here—books we thoroughly enjoyed that sparked wonderful discussions. And just because we didn't like a book, doesn't mean your group won't.

Key:

MG = middle grade (ages 8 to 12)

YA = young adult (ages 12 and up)

AD = adult

GN = graphic novel

RR = good for reluctant readers

AR = good for advanced readers

SA = screen (movie/TV) adaptation

S = part of a series

ANOTHER NOTE ON PROBLEMATIC AUTHORS

A word of caution about any booklist: Over the years, our understanding of different books (both their content and the views or actions of their authors) can change. While we have tried to describe some of the things you might want to know about these books, we cannot flag all of the potential issues with every book or every author. As noted on page 11, some of the authors and books we've mentioned already and listed in the following chapters have been or may be accused of racism, sexual harassment, homophobia, and more. We are not intending to ignore these issues or advocating that you support these authors and their books. Instead, we are recommending that you do your own research about the books that you choose for your book club to make sure that the choice works well for your group. A quick web search can tell you a lot about a book or an author, how they have been received, and potential problems. See the references in Online Book Reviews and Lists on page 199 for more websites that offer book reviews and commentary.

Harry Potter and the Sorcerer's Stone by J. K. Rowling

Fantasy **MG** **AR** **SA** **S**

This was the very first book we read, and after eleven years, this masterpiece still holds the record for the highest rating from our group: a perfect ten from everyone! (Luci)

The Tower Treasure (Hardy Boys Book #1) by Franklin W. Dixon

Mystery **MG** **SA** **S**

Although written long ago (1927), the kids thought this Hardy Boys mystery was exciting. Several of them devoured the entire series after reading this first one. (Kristin) Original editions of many of early Hardy Boys books, including this one, contained racist language and characters. Modern reprintings have removed it, but may still have issues depending on the particular edition. Be aware of this history if you choose to read any of the older books, or pick a contemporary mystery from chapter 9 instead. (Michelle)

The Sign of the Beaver by Elizabeth George Speare

Historical Fiction (MG) (SA)

When we read this book back in 2008, we enjoyed it. But later we discovered the white author's depiction of Maine's Penobscot Indians was stereotypical, inaccurate, and offensive. A better choice for historical fiction written by a Native American author would be *How I Became a Ghost: A Choctaw Trail of Tears Story* by Tim Tingle. (Michelle)

Tales of a Fourth Grade Nothing by Judy Blume

Humor (MG) (RR) (S)

For every older sibling who was ever irritated by a younger sibling. Who can forget when poor Fudge swallows the turtle! (Michelle) Poor Fudge? More like poor Peter! (Dana) What about the poor turtle?! (Owen)

Rascal by Sterling North

Realistic Fiction (MG) (RR) (SA)

This memoir of a young boy and his pet raccoon was one of my favorites we read when the kids were young. If you liked *Where the Red Fern Grows*, read *Rascal*! (Dana)

Inside Out and Back Again by Thanhha Lai

Historical Fiction (MG) (RR)

Inspired by the author's own childhood immigration experience: Lai and her family fled Vietnam during the war and were refugees in Alabama. Told in free verse, this is a beautiful and surprisingly funny coming-of-age story about immigration and starting over, from a child's perspective. The adults and kids really enjoyed this one. (Michelle)

A Wrinkle in Time by Madeleine L'Engle

Sci-Fi (MG) (AR) (S)

The classic story of science-loving, tesseract-jumping Meg, who journeys across universes to rescue her missing

father. We read this when the kids were in second grade. In hindsight, we should have waited until they were older. While they got the plot, I think the deeper themes went over their heads. (Dana).

Alvin Ho: Allergic to Girls, School, and Other Scary Things by Lenore Look

Humor MG RR S

This is a book about a kid, Alvin Ho, who is afraid of everything—girls, elevators, and most of all school. Because of this, he never talks at school. At home, however, he is a superhero called Firecracker Man, a brother, and a "gentleman in training." This is a very enjoyable and humorous book to read. (Luci)

Warriors: Into the Wild by Erin Hunter

Fantasy MG RR S

This series about a cat society was hugely popular when we read it and most of our kids loved it, but personally, as a grown-up, I couldn't wait for the book to end! (Kristin) Our family has three cats and I still hated these books. (Michelle) Everyone hates on this book now, but in elementary school the Warrior books were where it was at. And they asked some important questions, like: "What are our cats really up to?" (Owen)

Joey Pigza Swallowed the Key by Jack Gantos

Humor MG RR S

This series is about a character with ADHD. The humor, action, and short chapters make it a great choice for reluctant readers. In fact, it was chosen by a reluctant reader in our group. It gave all the kids a good window into a different kind of brain. (Michelle)

Hatchet by Gary Paulsen

Adventure MG RR S

This a very interesting survival story about a kid who gets stuck in the woods after a plane crash and has to figure out how to survive in the wilderness. I really enjoyed it and I read it several times when I was younger. (Luci)

Artemis Fowl: The Graphic Novel by Eoin Colfer

Fantasy MG GN RR SA S

This is a graphic novel version of the first novel in the *Artemis Fowl* series, a great collection that combines magic and mystery masterfully. I really liked the whole series and I think it's good for younger kids. It can also spark some good discussion about wealth and ethics. (Ronan)

Bud, Not Buddy by Christopher Paul Curtis

Historical Fiction MG AR

Set in 1936 Flint, Michigan, ten-year-old Bud is a motherless runaway on the road searching for a father he's never met. It's an award-winning story, and Curtis's brilliant writing easily sucks kids in so that they don't ever realize they are learning about American history. We had a great talk about racism, Jim Crow laws, and American jazz. (Michelle)

Tale of Despereaux: The Graphic Novel by Matt Smith and David Tilton

Fantasy MG GN RR

This is a graphic novel version of an award-winning novel about a brave mouse who rescues a princess. It's a wonderful story, and the graphic novel version is an easier read than the novel for younger kids. (Owen)

How to Train Your Dragon by Cressida Cowell

Fantasy MG RR SA S

The story of a kid who finds and trains a dragon. We saw the movie after finishing the book, which was really fun. It's a good read for young kids who like fantasy. (Luci)

Sideways Stories from Wayside School by Louis Sachar

Humor MG RR S

This book will appeal to kids with an ironic sense of humor who can handle a satirical presentation of school life. It's funny and a really easy read, which is great for kids who don't yet love reading. Some parents might not love Sachar's less-than-flattering portrayal of adults, but I loved his over-the-top parody. (Ann)

Rapunzel's Revenge by Shannon Hale and Dean Hale

Fantasy MG GN RR S

This graphic novel is a Wild West take on Rapunzel with a strong female hero. It's a fun read, but I don't remember having much deep discussion about it. (Ronan)

Diary of a Wimpy Kid by Jeff Kinney

Humor MG RR SA S

When this book got picked I thought, "We're going to read *that*?" But then my boys ended up loving this series, and now I buy them the new one every year. (Dana) This book, along with the next five or six in the series, is a great depiction of middle school life. They're quick reads, and they're really funny and worth reading. (Dominic)

Hoot by Carl Hiaasen

Humor MG AR SA S

Hoot is a wacky, hilarious novel with very likeable characters that also deals with the clash between environmentalism and capitalism. (Owen)

The Lightning Thief by Rick Riordan

Fantasy MG AR SA S

This book and its sequels and spinoffs are essentially the only reason I know anything about Greek mythology. Pretty much everyone really liked it, as well. (Dominic)

Holes by Louis Sachar

Humor MG AR SA S

Holes is a good book with a lot of humor and an exciting plot. We read it a while ago but I remember really liking it. (Ronan)

Bridge to Terabithia
by Katherine Paterson

Realistic Fiction (MG) (AR) (SA)

This was one of my favorite books growing up, so I was nervous about suggesting it in case it didn't age well and the kids panned it. It turned out OK—it was interesting to read again as an adult and it prompted a good discussion about a very sad topic. (Kristin)

Becoming Naomi León
by Pam Muñoz Ryan

Realistic Fiction (MG) (AR)

A beautifully written story of a young Mexican American girl coming of age and discovering her identity amid poverty and family challenges. I greatly enjoy the writing of Pam Muñoz Ryan and found it to be a very compelling read. (Owen)

Where the Red Fern Grows
by Wilson Rawls

Adventure (MG) (AR) (SA)

This is one of my favorite books of all time and the only one that makes me cry every time I read it. (Owen) I loved this book! It's a great story of friendship between a boy and his dogs. It also made me cry when I read it. (Ronan)

Heck: Where the Bad Kids Go
by Dale E. Basye

Humor (MG) (AR) (S)

Our kids enjoyed the pun-filled humor and the after-death-by-marshmallow-explosion storyline. A good pick for kids who like *Diary of a Wimpy Kid*. (Michelle)

Because of Winn-Dixie
by Kate DiCamillo

Realistic Fiction (MG) (RR) (SA)

A sweet, humorous tale of a young girl spending the summer with her newfound best friend and dog, Winn-Dixie. The story deals with deeper issues of family and friendship that can lead to a good discussion for younger readers. (Owen)

One-Handed Catch by M. J. Auch

Sports MG AR

This book is about a kid who lost his hand when he was young but still plays baseball. I really liked it because it's about sports. It was a good book to talk about because it is about someone overcoming adversity. (Luci)

I, Q: Independence Hall by Roland Smith

Mystery MG RR S

This book was surprisingly good for being a fairly generic spy book. I read the next few books in the series because I enjoyed the fast-paced action. (Dominic)

Out of My Mind by Sharon Draper

Realistic Fiction MG AR

A book about a girl with cerebral palsy who can't walk or talk but has a photographic memory. (The author doesn't have cerebral palsy herself, but her daughter does.) It's interesting, well written, and shines a light on what it's like to live with a disability. (Luci) Although we were young, this book inspired an interesting discussion about how people with disabilities function in a society built to overlook them. (Owen)

The True Confessions of Charlotte Doyle by Avi

Historical Fiction MG AR

One of my favorite heroines ever—Charlotte the bad-ass pirate! A great book to settle any boy book/girl book debate. *All* kids love this story. At least all of ours did. (Michelle)

When You Reach Me by Rebecca Stead

Sci-Fi MG AR

Another great heroine in a cool, time-bending sci-fi story set in the 1970s. Inspired by *A Wrinkle in Time*, it shares a lot of what's wonderful about that book. (Michelle)

The Search for WondLa by Tony DiTerlizzi

Fantasy MG RR S

Short chapters, lots of illustrations, and an exciting sci-fi story, this book is great for younger readers who love fantasy adventures. It's also got a great heroine and incredible art by Caldecott winner DiTerlizzi. (Michelle)

The Birchbark House by Louise Erdrich

Historical Fiction   S

Told from the perspective of a young Ojibwa girl living on an island in Lake Superior in 1847 as she and her community deal with the dangerous newcomers to their land. Set around the same time and location as Laura Ingalls Wilder's Little House on the Prairie series, this book tells a powerful story from the point of view of the Indigenous people. Erdrich's own Ojibwa ancestry adds to the truth and power of the book. (Michelle)

Leviathan by Scott Westerfeld

Sci-Fi YA AR S

Leviathan is an alternate history of World War I with genetic engineering and giant robots. What's not to love? This is a really unique and well-written book that captivates the reader. A good read for history buffs *and* sci-fi lovers. (Ronan)

Johnny Tremain by Esther Forbes

Historical Fiction   SA

The classic tale of a fourteen-year-old silversmith who gets pulled into the American Revolution. It's one of my childhood favorites, so I was excited to share it with the group. If you like historical fiction, or your kids are studying US history, it's a good choice. (Dana)

Fablehaven by Brandon Mull

Fantasy MG RR S

This book, about two siblings who discover a secret refuge for magical creatures, inspired one adult in the group (me) to read the whole series. It has really positive female characters and a nice balance between adventure and character development. (Ann)

The 39 Clues: The Maze of Bones by Rick Riordan

Mystery   S

This book was the first and best in the long 39 Clues series, one of Rick Riordan's earliest. (Later books in the series were written by different authors.) It's about two orphans who have to solve the mystery of their parents' disappearance. It is full of secret codes for readers to decipher. (Dominic)

The Hobbit by J. R. R. Tolkien

Fantasy MG SA S

I worried this book wouldn't stand the test of time, but it did. It's action-packed, has short chapters full of hobbits, dwarves, and elves, plus lots of cool monsters and magic. The kids loved it, and it was fun to discuss a book from the parents' childhoods. (Michelle)

The Graveyard Book by Neil Gaiman

Fantasy MG/ YA GN AR

Neil Gaiman is a great writer, and he constructs a really good story here. It's basically a retelling of *The Jungle Book*, but set in a cemetery, with ghosts. (Ronan) I read this book when I was really young and was bored because I didn't understand it. When I read it for book club a few years later I enjoyed it a lot more. (Dominic)

Small Steps: The Year I Got Polio by Peg Kehret

Memoir MG AR

A true story of the author's battle with polio when she was twelve years old, was paralyzed, and had to move to a polio ward for treatment. What could be a sad, boring story was actually one of the most gripping and humorous books we read. The kids loved it and we had a wonderful talk about what it would be like to live in a time when diseases like polio were a real threat. Our kids didn't realize their grandparents grew up with the risk of getting polio. Post-COVID, it would be even more interesting to discuss. (Michelle)

Found: The Missing, Book 1 by Margaret Peterson Haddix

Sci-Fi MG S

This book is the start of a series of time travel–based adventures, which, while not particularly thought-provoking, were definitely entertaining. The author was one of my favorite middle grade authors, and I read a lot of her books. (Dominic)

The Invention of Hugo Cabret by Brian Selznick

Fantasy MG RR SA

I really liked this book. It's a mix of graphic novel pages and regular prose and is about a young boy living in a clock tower inside a Paris train station. It's a cool but strange book and might not appeal to everyone. (Ronan)

The Stonekeeper (Amulet Book 1) by Kazu Kibuishi

Fantasy MG GN RR S

The Amulet series is one of the best graphic novel series I've ever read. This first story is about two siblings who have to rescue their mom from an evil underground world full of demons, robots, and talking animals. The universe is unlike any other and the creativity in these books is just amazing. (Ronan)

The Incredible Journey by Sheila Burnford

Fantasy MG RR SA

The story of two dogs and a cat who journey cross-country to find their

owners. A good story, but none of us could remember many details. So, not terribly memorable. (Owen)

Wonder by R. J. Palacio

Realistic Fiction MG RR SA S

This is the story of August, a fifth grader with facial differences who goes to school for the first time. We had a really fascinating discussion about it. The kids read it when they were ten, the perfect age to be thinking about kids who are different. It brought up some really interesting questions, and the kids challenged themselves to think about how they might react in similar situations. An excellent book club choice for kids and parents. (Ann) This is one of the best realistic fiction books I have ever read! (Ronan)

Refugee by Alan Gratz

Realistic Fiction MG AR

Three stories of incredible, dangerous journeys made this a page-turner, and gave us good material to talk about the refugee crisis in the world today and how government policies affect immigrants. (Noah)

The Giver by Lois Lowry

Sci-Fi (MG) (GN) (AR) (SA) (S)

A "classic" dystopian book, it is set in a world of total conformity and dark secrets. We had a good discussion about what happens when you structure society too much. (Noah) While this book has some obvious discussion points that might make it a good book club book, it wasn't one of my favorites in terms of reading for pleasure. (Dominic)

Code Talker: A Novel about the Navajo Marines of World War Two by Joseph Bruchac

Historical Fiction (MG) / (YA)

This book is about a group of Navajo Marines who use their language to create unbreakable codes during World War II. This was a really informative and well-written book. It's a unique story that provides a different perspective on the war. I thought it was really cool to learn more about how codes were used and how the Navajo helped win the war. (Ronan)

The Book Thief by Marcus Zusak

Historical Fiction (YA) (AR) (SA)

This is an amazing book. The book's unique narrator, Death, tells the story of Liesel, a German girl living through World War II. It was a very deep and emotional story. (Ronan) I found the different narrators confusing, but watching the movie afterward helped. (Noah)

Ender's Game by Orson Scott Card

Sci-Fi (YA) / (AD) (AR) (SA) (S)

This was a great sci-fi novel about a future where governments breed and train child soldiers. (Noah) This is easily in my top ten sci-fi books ever. You become very attached to the main character and the plot is amazing. The entire book is incredibly well written. I think this book really paved the way for future sci-fi books since we enjoyed it so much. There are also lots of options for great discussion with this book. (Ronan)

Keeper by Mal Peet

Fantasy/Sports YA RR

My nephew, who was a reluctant reader and avid soccer player, turned me on to this book. It's a beautifully told story combining sports and mystical realism. (Dana) I liked this one because I like books about sports. It's not a normal book about sports, which made it a more unique and interesting read. (Luci)

The Hunger Games by Suzanne Collins

Sci-Fi YA RR SA S

One of the most famous dystopian novels, it's about Katniss Everdeen, who must fight to the death for her family and district in her world's televised "Hunger Games." I really like this book and the whole series—it is one of my favorite dystopian books of all time. Pretty much everyone liked it, but it was the first really intense book we read and there was a lot we really wanted to talk about. It was a milestone in our book club. (Luci)

Whirligig by Paul Fleischman

Realistic Fiction YA AR

Told from the point of view of several characters, *Whirligig* is a tale of redemption, exploring how one person's actions can impact the lives of many. Great story! I used to read this book with my sixth grade students. Our group really enjoyed it as well. (Dana)

Unwind by Neal Shusterman

Sci-Fi YA AR S

An immersive story that keeps you wanting more. *Unwind* has a disturbing premise—abortion is illegal in the future, but parents may choose to "unwind" their teens, donating their parts to others in need. This dark, captivating dystopian series is great for sci-fi lovers. It also has tons of ethical dilemmas that made for an excellent discussion. (Ronan)

The Fault in Our Stars by John Green

Realistic Fiction YA AR SA

Both kids and adults in our group thoroughly enjoyed this book, a love story about two teens with cancer. We also watched the movie, which had a few awkward moments for the teens (watching sex scenes with parents!). (Kristin) An emotionally captivating novel that I was surprised to discover I liked. (Noah)

The Eyes of the Dragon by Stephen King

Fantasy AD AR

Though it was written for adults, it was a good read for teens as well. A rare fantasy novel by the king of horror, it focuses on two rival princes and their struggle for power in a magical world. We thought it was OK, but not incredible. I may read it again now that I am older to see if I like it more. (Dominic)

The Maze Runner by James Dashner

Sci-Fi YA RR SA S

A dystopian novel about a boy who wakes up with no memory and inside a deadly maze he must fight to escape. It was enjoyable but failed to offer much substance or large themes for a good group discussion. (Owen) This novel

kept me captivated from the first to the last page. I think it's a great read set in a very interesting world. (Ronan)

The Outsiders by S. E. Hinton

Realistic Fiction YA SA

A story of the haves versus the have-nots, set in the 1950s. Great characters, captivating plot, and interesting theme about the class divide all made for a good discussion. (Noah) I loved this book. The writing felt raw and emotional, and it was a great classic to discuss. (Ronan) Another book that surprised me in how well it stood the test of time. The kids loved it, even though it was written in 1967. They related to the characters' emotions and struggles, a testament to the brilliant writing of fifteen-year-old S. E. Hinton. (Michelle)

Feed by M. T. Anderson

Sci-Fi YA AR

This dystopian story is set in a future where everyone has computers built into their brains. It has a lot of good discussion topics because it seems like a very possible future and it's interesting to discuss the pros and cons of technology, social media, and so on. (Ronan)

Don't Care High
by Gordon Korman

Realistic Fiction YA RR

Two new students try to bring school spirit to a high school where it's non-existent. It was hard to find a print version of this 1985 book, but there's an e-book. It's pretty funny and similar to a lot of Gordon Korman's more recent, better-known books. (Dominic)

Into Thin Air: A Personal
Account of the Mt. Everest
Disaster by Jon Krakauer

Nonfiction YA / AD AR SA

I chose this book, and most of the group liked it. It's adult nonfiction but has an exciting plot full of adventure and danger. I liked the descriptions of the Himalayas and the climbing culture. (Noah) This book kept me on the edge of my seat. It's an exciting story of climbing Everest and the perils of that journey. I didn't know much about climbing, so this was a super interesting book for me. (Ronan)

Lord of the Flies
by William Golding

Realistic Fiction YA / AD AR SA

A plane full of young boys crashes on a deserted island, where they must create their own rules and society and fend for themselves. I think about the themes in this book a lot. I liked the plot and the commentary on human nature. (Noah) Often the classics don't end up being as good as they are made out to be. But in this case, I really enjoyed *Lord of the Flies* and definitely understand why it is still being read sixty-plus years later. (Owen)

The Running Dream
by Wendelin Van Draanen

Realistic Fiction YA

This is the story of a runner who loses her leg and hopes to run again with a new prosthetic. I enjoyed the book a lot. The characters were well written and the story inspiring. (Dominic)

Survival (Alpha Force Book 1) by Chris Ryan

Adventure YA RR S

A survival story about five kids marooned on a desert island, where they face Komodo dragons, sharks, pirates, and more. While this wasn't my or anyone's favorite book, it does have some redeeming value: The author has a lot of military experience, so the survival situations were fairly realistic. (Dominic)

Ready Player One by Ernest Cline

Sci-Fi YA / AD AR SA S

A futuristic, dystopian *Charlie and the Chocolate Factory*, about an eccentric video game inventor who dies and leaves his fortune to whoever can solve his puzzle. The adults loved this one since it was filled with 1980s music and allowed us to loudly reminisce as the kids tried to discuss the book and its literary merits. (Ann) The book's setting is unlike any other and the adventure story keeps you coming back for more. This is in my top five favorite books of all time. (Ronan) I think this has the most votes for Favorite Book in our group—tying the almost insurmountable *Harry Potter*! (Michelle)

Touching the Void by Joe Simpson

Nonfiction YA / AD AR SA

This incredible survival story about two mountaineers in the Peruvian Andes is a good portrayal of rock climbing culture. We had a great discussion about whether they made the right choices and what we would do if it was us. (Noah) While I liked the similar story of *Into Thin Air*, I felt this book went too far into the mechanics of climbing. For someone who isn't that into climbing, it dragged at times. (Dominic)

The Absolutely True Diary of a Part-Time Indian by Sherman Alexie

Realistic Fiction YA RR

Based on Alexie's real life, it tells the story of a Native teen living on a reservation who leaves to go to an all-white farm-town school. This book was funny but also touched on deep societal issues. (Noah) Alexie's unique sense of humor combined with his commentary on racism, identity, and acceptance produced a quirky, hilarious read that was universally enjoyed by our group and sparked a great discussion. (Owen)

The 5th Wave by Rick Yancey

Sci-Fi (YA) (SA) (S)

Earth has been invaded by aliens in four different waves, leaving few human survivors. One of them, Cassie, must leave her hiding spot to find her little brother. Although it wasn't the best book I've ever read, it was still enjoyable. (Ronan)

Challenger Deep by Neal Shusterman, illustrated by Brendan Shusterman

Realistic Fiction (YA) (AR)

This story, about a teen with mental illness, is told in alternating realistic and fantasy storylines that weave together nicely. Co-created with his son, Brendan, who has schizophrenia and did the artwork for the book, Shusterman's story led our group to a deep and challenging discussion around mental illness. (Owen)

To Kill a Mockingbird by Harper Lee

Realistic Fiction (YA)/(AD) (AR) (SA)

This classic didn't hold up well for our 2017 reading, and there has been a lot of discussion about its appropriateness since it is about racism, but told from an entirely white point of view. A fantastic "classic" replacement for teens that also dives into Black history and racial inequality, but from a Black point of view, is *The Autobiography of Malcolm X* by Alex Haley. Although written for adults, teens will enjoy it. (Michelle)

The Knife of Never Letting Go by Patrick Ness

Sci-Fi (YA) (SA) (S)

The story takes place in a world where all women are dead, and the thoughts of men and animals can be heard aloud as Noise. Although it's another dystopian book (which we read a lot of), I would say this was one of the better ones. The book drew me in and led to some interesting discussion. It also got pretty high ratings from most people. (Dominic)

A Long Walk to Water
by Linda Sue Park

Realistic Fiction MG RR

A short but powerful read about two kids living very different lives in Africa. It prompted great discussions about teens in other cultures, refugees, and current events. I was surprised at how much discussion we got out of such a small book. (Kristin)

A Study in Charlotte
by Brittany Cavallaro

Mystery YA RR S

This book takes the stories of Sherlock Holmes and puts them in a posh, New England boarding school with Charlotte Holmes, Holmes's great-great-great granddaughter, on the case. The novel is fun and witty, with plenty of twists and turns. It also has lots of references to Doyle's books to keep Sherlock Holmes fans happy. (Owen)

Every Day by David Levithan

Realistic Fiction YA SA S

This book has an interesting premise—the main character switches bodies every day, inhabiting different genders and sexual orientations—which led to a great discussion about gender and attraction. It's also a love story, so people who like romance will like this book. I highly recommend it. (Ronan) Although I'm not a romance fan, the character switching bodies made it interesting enough that I enjoyed reading it. (Dominic)

A Separate Peace
by John Knowles

Historical Fiction YA / AD AR SA

This classic novel, about two male friends at a New England boarding school during World War II, was a story I read in high school. I enjoyed reading it again, but it got mixed reviews from the kids. (Dana)

When Nobody Was Watching
by Carli Lloyd

Memoir YA RR

Luci chose this memoir by soccer star Carli Lloyd because she is a big women's soccer fan. It led to a great discussion about perseverance in sports and life. The non-sports fans were good "sports" about reading it. (Kristin) It was interesting to read about such an iconic athlete. Lloyd suffered many setbacks and showed that becoming a top-level athlete is never easy. (Noah)

The Radius of Us
by Marie Marquardt

Realistic Fiction YA

This story is told in alternating voices: Gretchen, a white girl dealing with the trauma of being assaulted, and Phoenix, a recent immigrant from El Salvador, dealing with the traumas of his past and present. Their unlikely friendship changes them both. Many of us liked this book and it led to a good discussion about immigration and trauma. (Luci)

The Cure for Dreaming
by Cat Winters

Fantasy YA AR

The premise—exploring the world of hypnosis against the historical background of the suffrage movement of 1900—greatly intrigued me, but I felt the execution fell short as the book struggled to decide if it wanted to be realistic or fantastical. I felt there was never a consistent tone or direction. (Owen)

The Perks of Being a Wallflower
by Stephen Chbosky

Realistic Fiction YA AR SA

Dark, depressing, but also quite funny, *The Perks of Being a Wallflower* received a mixed bag of reviews. Some enjoyed the realistic portrayals and difficult themes, others found it hard to read. It is one of my favorite books. (Owen) I loved this book and felt it was spot-on in its portrayal of the challenges of being a teenager and finding your way. (Dana)

Insignia by S. J. Kincaid

Sci-Fi YA S

Set in World War III, when Earth's resources are nearly gone and fighting will determine who gets what's left. The hero is a VR gamer who could save the world. Although a typical dystopian novel, it was still thought-provoking. (Luci) *Insignia* offered little new insight on the world as a whole—something I believe a good dystopian novel should do. (Owen)

I'll Give You the Sun by Jandy Nelson

Realistic Fiction

Told in the alternating voices of a twin brother and sister, this book is unusual in that it tells two love stories, one heterosexual and one same-sex. A great choice for fans of YA writers like David Levithan, John Green, and Rainbow Rowell. (Michelle)

The Hate U Give by Angie Thomas

Realistic Fiction **YA** **SA** **S**

This is very moving novel about a young Black girl who witnesses her friend getting shot by the police and must decide what to do about it. It was an illuminating window into the racism and violence inflicted on Black Americans that, as a white boy, I hadn't previously understood. It's a super well-written book with an awesome main character. (Ronan) Out of all the books I've read, I was the most emotionally moved by this one. The stark portrayal of race issues in America today, as well as the author's ability to get us to care about the characters, made this book feel very real. (Noah)

Uglies by Scott Westerfeld

Sci-Fi **YA** **GN** **RR** **S**

This book is about a dystopian society in which all sixteen-year-olds get an operation to make them "pretty." The main character, Tally, can't wait for her surgery. But when Tally finds a friend who refused the surgery and ran away, she discovers that the surgery alters teens' *minds* as well. And not in a good way. *Uglies* sparked good discussions about the societal pressures of being pretty and the need for people to conform. I really liked it. The premise is unlike any other dystopian novel I've read (Ronan).

Ten by Gretchen McNeil

Mystery **YA** **RR** **SA**

A murder mystery inspired by Agatha Christie's classic *And Then There Were None*. Ten teens are invited to party in a mansion on an island, where they are picked off one by one. This was our first murder mystery in book club and everyone enjoyed it. The discussion was OK, but it wasn't the best book for discussing deep issues. (Luci)

March Book 1, March Book 2, and March Book 3 by John Lewis

Historical Fiction (YA) (GN) (AR) (S)

This graphic novel trilogy presents some of the most pivotal moments of the civil rights movement in an incredibly captivating manner. A memoir by the late Senator John Lewis, the books powerfully illustrate the horrors inflicted on Black people while advocating for their rights in the 1950s and 1960s. Sparked a fascinating group discussion. (Owen)

Daughter of Smoke & Bone by Laini Taylor

Fantasy (YA) (AR) (S)

This is one of the best fantasy books I have ever read. Karou collects human teeth for her monster caretakers, but she has no childhood memories and doesn't know her own identity until a mysterious stranger forces her to investigate. The universe is amazing, and anybody who likes fantasy at all will love it. It is an absolute must-read, in my top five favorite books of all time. (Ronan) I typically do not like fantasy, but I loved this story. I was hooked from the beginning. (Dana)

All the Bright Places by Jennifer Niven

Realistic Fiction (YA) (SA)

A love story about two suicidal teens who meet and try to save each other. Despite it being a relationship story, I found it surprisingly enjoyable. Books with romance are not my thing, but this was different because it touched on interesting issues like depression and cliques. We had a good discussion about mental health in our society. (Noah)

The Hitchhiker's Guide to the Galaxy by Douglas Adams

Sci-Fi (YA) /(AD) (AR) (SA)

This cult classic is about a human whisked into outer space by his alien friend, thus escaping Earth's destruction and embarking on a search for the meaning of life. It appealed to some of the kids, but not all. It seems to be aging well for those kids who have an ironic sense of humor or are fans of *Doctor Who*. (Ann)

Simon vs. the Homo Sapiens Agenda by Becky Albertalli

Realistic Fiction YA RR SA

I thought this story, about a closeted gay teen falling in love and coming out to friends and family, was funny and relatable. It was also emotionally powerful and provided a perspective that I, for one, did not know about. A great book for group discussion. (Noah)

Dance of the Infidels: A Portrait of Bud Powell by Francis Paudras

Biography AD AR

This book details 1940s bebop jazz musician Bud Powell's mental health challenges and how Black people were treated in America versus Paris. Unfortunately, most people in our book club were put off by the author's amateur writing and the book's slow start. (Noah) Noah loved this book. Jazz is his thing. The rest of us were confused by the bad writing. That said, we still had a really good discussion about racism and the connections between creativity, addiction, and mental illness. (Owen)

1984 by George Orwell

Sci-Fi YA / AD AR SA

Though published in 1949, it was scary to see how many of the author's fears about the totalitarianism, repression, and mass surveillance of World War II still ring true today. Our discussion for this novel covered many of our concerns about modern society. (Owen) It reinforced why I don't want to have an Alexa in my home! (Dana)

Tweak by Nic Sheff

Memoir YA AR SA

As a parent, I wondered if the kids could handle this book's content, which was shocking in its stark portrayal of the depths of drug addiction. The kids handled it with maturity and recognized that the author was trying to show all the ugliness of an addict's life without editing for his audience. (Lissa) This was one of the best discussions I've been a part of in the book club. We talked candidly about drug addiction, mental health, family dynamics, and factors that might lead to drug addiction. (Noah)

Circe by Madeline Miller

Fantasy (AD) (AR) (S)

I have always greatly enjoyed Greek mythology: My parents read me stories of Daedalus and Persephone when I was young and I loved Percy Jackson in elementary school. *Circe* was an excellent updated retelling of the ancient stories about Circe the witch and her interactions with many Greek heroes. (Owen)

Panic by Lauren Oliver

Realistic Fiction (YA)

In Carp, all graduating seniors play a high-risk game called Panic for its $50,000 prize and the chance to escape their small town. While *Panic* may not have been the deepest book we've read, it was engaging and fun to read. It raised a few interesting questions about risk taking and how the behavior of teens is portrayed in the media. (Dominic)

This Time Will Be Different by Misa Sugiura

Realistic Fiction (YA) (AR)

The story of a Japanese-American girl who works in her aunt's flower shop until it's sold to a white family that took advantage of her ancestors in World War II, when they were sent to internment camps. This book sparked good discussion about race and showed how past events can continue to influence the future. (Ronan) I thought this book gave good insight into the culture of Japanese immigrants. (Dominic)

Monday's Not Coming by Tiffany Jackson

Realistic Fiction (YA)

In this story about the disappearance of a young Black girl, the author switches between a thoughtful exploration of the flaws in US social work and policing and a thriller, making the book feel like it lacks focus. The language seemed to be written for a younger, middle-school audience despite depicting some very graphic, adult imagery. (Owen)

Unbroken (The Young Adult Adaptation): An Olympian's Journey from Airman to Castaway to Captive by Laura Hillenbrand

Biography YA RR SA

A nonfiction World War II memoir about a former Olympic track star who survived a plane crash over the Pacific, spent forty-seven days drifting in a lifeboat, only to be captured and held in a brutal Japanese POW camp for three years. This book led to a lot of good discussion about the war on the Pacific Front, which is an aspect of World War II we didn't know much about. We also talked about the treatment of POWs, and what humanitarian rules there should be in war. (Dominic)

Trevor Noah: Born a Crime: Stories from a South African Childhood (The Young Adult Adaptation) by Trevor Noah

Memoir YA RR

I have been a fan of Trevor Noah's stand-up for a while, so it was interesting to learn about his difficult past and how it was to grow up biracial in apartheid South Africa. He has a distinct, humorous voice that makes reading his memoir very enjoyable and brings some comedy to heavy topics. (Ronan) There is a YA and an adult version of this book. Both are great. The story and Trevor Noah's excellent writing will hook both teens and adult readers. This is a great choice for parents and kids. (Michelle)

Chapter 9

One Hundred More Books We Love (But Didn't Read in Book Club)

"You still have a lot of time to make yourself be what you want. There's still a lot of good in the world."

—from *The Outsiders* by S. E. Hinton

ADVENTURES AND JOURNEYS

The Bridge Home
by Padma Venkatraman

Realistic Fiction

Eleven-year-old runaway Viji and her sister Rukku find friendship and safety with homeless boys Muthi and Arul. The group spends their days on the streets in Chennai, India, learning to survive on their own. The children are faced with a challenge when one of their group may need more help than they can provide.

Counting by 7s by Holly
Goldberg Sloan

Realistic Fiction MG AR

Willow Chance is a twelve-year-old girl obsessed with numbers (especially sevens) and medical conditions. Her adoptive parents tragically die in the opening of the book, so Willow sets out on a quest to establish connections after her world falls apart. Good for discussions about being different and finding ways to fit in.

Firekeeper's Daughter
by Angeline Boulley

Realistic Fiction YA AR

Daunis is an Ojibwe teen who witnesses a murder tied to a deadly new drug being used by Native tribes and dives into the FBI investigation by going undercover. Daunis dates, plays hockey, and uses both traditional medicine and western science in her detective work with the FBI. This tense thriller features a fully fleshed out Indigenous hero written by an Ojibwe author and, though fictional, highlights the present-day experience of Indigenous people in America.

I Am Still Alive by Kate
Alice Marshall

Realistic Fiction

After her mother is killed in a car crash, Jess is sent to live with her father in the Canadian wilderness. She doesn't know him very well, and her situation worsens when he is murdered. Jess and her father's dog, Bo, must fend for themselves in the wilderness and find a way out. A thrilling novel for kids who enjoy survival adventures.

Internment by Samira Ahmed

Sci-Fi YA RR

A dystopian novel set in a terrifying, Trumpian America where seventeen-year-old Layla and her parents are forced into an internment camp for Muslim American citizens. With the help of new friends inside the camp and a boyfriend outside, Layla fights for her freedom. This gripping story highlights the ignorance and hatred behind Islamophobia, challenging readers to question silence and complicity.

King and the Dragonflies by Kacen Callender

Realistic Fiction MG AR

This short but powerful novel is set in the Louisiana bayou. Twelve-year-old King's brother has died. When he finds his former best friend, Sandy, hiding in his backyard, King decides to help him and learns about himself in the process. The book explores some difficult subjects like grief, homophobia, and identity in a moving first-person voice.

One Came Home by Amy Timberlake

Historical Fiction MG

A mystery/adventure novel involving a family in late nineteenth-century Wisconsin. Georgie's sister, Agatha, runs off with a group tracing a pigeon migration. When the sheriff finds a dead body dressed in Agatha's clothes, everyone assumes the worst. Georgie doesn't believe it's her sister and sets out to find the truth. A page-turner full of humor, friendship, and inspiration.

Percy Jackson and the Olympians series by Rick Riordan

Fantasy MG RR SA S

A popular series of fantasy adventure novels inspired by Greek mythology. The main character, Percy Jackson, is a "half-blood," with one human parent and the other a Greek god. Throughout the series, he and his friends encounter many characters from Greek myths, some helpful, and some not so much. The books are exciting and quite funny, and after finishing, readers will know a lot more about Greek mythology than they did before.

Where the Mountain Meets the Moon by Grace Lin

Fantasy `MG` `AR`

Inspired by the Chinese folklore she heard as a child, Grace Lin's fantasy-adventure novel tells of ten-year-old Minli's quest to find the Old Man of the Moon, who she believes will bring good fortune to her family and village. Along the way, she frees a trapped dragon who joins her on her quest. The story culminates with a test of Minli's loyalty to her new friend.

The Whispers by Greg Howard

Realistic Fiction `MG`

This is a moving story about Riley, an eleven-year-old LGBTQ+ boy who believes that magical creatures, the Whispers, will grant his wishes. Riley embarks on an adventure to find them. The wish he wants most is for his mom to come home. This emotional story will make you laugh and cry as it addresses issues of sexuality, loss, friendship, and self-acceptance.

FRIENDSHIP AND ROMANCE

Cemetery Boys by Aiden Thomas

Fantasy `YA`

Sixteen-year-old transgender protagonist Yadriel tries to summon the ghost of his murdered cousin to help him prove his gender identity to his conservative family. Instead, he accidentally calls up the ghost of Julian Diaz, who has some loose ends he has left behind in life. He won't leave unless Yadriel helps him to solve the mystery of his death. On his quest to help Julian, Yadriel gains understanding about his own Latinx identity.

Eleanor & Park by Rainbow Rowell

Realistic Fiction `YA`

First love is hard enough, but it's even harder when it's between outsiders. This rich novel navigates the challenges of high school love between two awkward teens: a chubby, unpopular girl and her nerdy, half-Korean half-white boyfriend. It deals unflinchingly with mature themes like bullying and abuse. Set in the 1980s, Gen-X readers are sure to enjoy the musical references.

The First Rule of Punk
by Celia C. Pérez

Realistic Fiction (MG)

Twelve-year-old Malú loves skate-boarding and rock-and-roll. As she starts at a new middle school, she blazes her own path, forming a band filled with other kids who don't fit in. A story about friendship, discovering who you are, and standing up for yourself.

If I Ever Get Out of Here
by Eric Gansworth

Realistic Fiction (YA) (RR)

Set in 1975, this is a story of friendship between two very different boys. Lewis is poor and lives on the Tuscarora Indian reservation. George is white, lives on the Air Force base, and is comfortably middle-class. Their shared love of music, especially the Beatles, bonds them, but other differences threaten to tear their friendship apart. Any kid wrestling with friendship issues will relate, and it will spark great group discussions.

The Love and Lies of Rukhsana Ali
by Sabina Khan

Realistic Fiction (YA)

Rukhsana comes from a conservative family that she desperately wants to get away from. She plans to go to Caltech to become an engineer, but when her Muslim parents catch her kissing her girlfriend Ariana, everything changes. She is forced to move to Bangladesh, where being gay is not accepted. A powerful, moving story about Rukhsana's fight to be herself and keep her love, while keeping her family as well. This Muslim author is not queer, but she wrote the story for her daughter, who is.

The Penderwicks
by Jeanne Birdsall

Realistic Fiction (MG) (AR) (S)

When the Penderwick sisters learn they will spend the summer at a cottage in the country, they are unsure what to expect. To their delight, they find a sprawling estate ripe for summertime adventures. While the grouchy property owner, Mrs. Tifton, tries to thwart their fun, her son, Jeffrey, becomes an eager accomplice and a friend. A funny, modern update on classic kids' books like *The Secret Garden* and *Anne of Green Gables*.

Piecing Me Together
by Renée Watson

Realistic Fiction (MG)/(YA)

This is a powerful story about Jade, a young Black girl determined to succeed. After transferring to a predominantly white private school, Jade befriends a white girl from her neighborhood who is navigating some of the same issues. The book beautifully addresses issues of poverty, race, privilege, stereotypes, friendship, and identity as their friendship grows and changes, and as Jade finds her voice through art.

The Sun Is Also a Star
by Nicola Yoon

Realistic Fiction (YA) (SA)

A romantic coming-of-age story that takes place all on one very hectic day. Natasha is rushing to help her family avoid deportation, and Daniel is struggling with the academic expectations of his immigrant parents versus his own passions. As they meet and discover young love on the streets of New York City, they also wrestle with issues related to interracial relationships and immigration, and the irrationality of love at first sight.

The Season of Styx Malone
by Kekla Magoon

Realistic Fiction (MG) (RR)

In search of adventure, two brothers, Caleb (aged ten) and Bobby Gene (aged eleven), befriend their cool sixteen-year-old neighbor, Styx Malone. When they join Styx's money-making scheme, their misadventure tests the brothers' sense of what's right and helps them discover that all is not always as it seems.

They Both Die at the End
by Adam Silvera

Realistic Fiction (YA)

In this book, both Mateo and Rufus are told they are going to die that day. They are complete strangers, but through the app Last Friend, they both make one last friend in each other. This book follows their adventures through one last unforgettable day.

HUMOR

An Abundance of Katherines by John Green

Realistic Fiction YA AR

Colin is a genius who has dated nineteen girls named Katherine. It has never gone well, and Colin wants to figure out why. On a road trip with his best friend, he creates a formula to predict how compatible two people are. A funny yet poignant book about love and friendship. And math. One of John Green's funniest novels.

American Panda by Gloria Chao

Realistic Fiction YA

After skipping a grade at her Taiwanese parents' insistence, seventeen-year-old Mei is a freshman at MIT. Her parents have planned out her future: medical degree, Taiwanese husband of status, and children. In her own very funny voice, Mei expresses her doubts about the path her parents have chosen for her. After a renewed connection to her estranged brother, she has more questions than ever about what she really wants.

Big Nate series by Lincoln Peirce

Realistic Fiction MG RR S

This is a popular illustrated series about sixth grader Nate and his hilarious misadventures. Nate and his friends are a quirky, relatable group who are expertly depicted with unique characteristics that bring them to life and keep readers engaged.

Captain Underpants series by Dav Pilkey

Realistic Fiction MG RR SA S

George and Harold are the biggest pranksters in the fourth grade. But after getting caught, they hypnotize the principal, turning him into superhero Captain Underpants. Captain Underpants fights crime, battling a series of underwear-themed enemies. A ridiculous and hilarious book series that will appeal to many elementary schoolers and reluctant readers.

Dork Diaries series
by Rachel Renée Russell

Realistic Fiction MG RR S

Written for all the unpopular kids in middle school (weren't we all?), this highly illustrated series follows the misadventures of Nikki as she navigates the trials and terrors of middle school: dealing with mean girls, finding the right clothes, crushes, and making friends. With over fifteen books and counting, this series will keep readers busy.

The Field Guide to the
North American Teenager
by Ben Philippe

Realistic Fiction YA

Norris, a smart, funny Black French Canadian, moves to Austin, Texas, and must contend with American high school clichés he's only ever seen in John Hughes movies—from football players to cheerleaders to Manic Pixie Dreamgirls. As he figures out first love, first job, and a long-distance BFF, Norris discovers it may not be Texas causing him trouble, but his own hang-ups. A funny, heartfelt book for fans of Nicola Yoon and John Green.

Flora and Ulysses
by Kate DiCamillo

Fantasy MG RR

A laugh-out-loud novel about ten-year-old Flora, who befriends a squirrel named Ulysses after he is sucked into a vacuum cleaner and develops superpowers. Ulysses begins writing poetry on a typewriter and becomes the intermediary between Flora and her divorcing parents. A novel of friendship, acceptance, and the power of communication—one of Kate DiCamillo's funniest novels ever.

It Ain't So Awful, Falafel
by Firoozeh Dumas

Realistic Fiction MG

Inspired by the author's own experience growing up Iranian in the United States during the Islamic Revolution and Iranian Hostage Crisis. Zomorod, who calls herself "Cindy" to assimilate, must navigate the challenges of middle school, bullies, and immigrant parents. With humor and compassion, this story gives dimension to the experience of families caught between the life they left behind and the life they hope to build in their new country.

Not So Pure and Simple
by Lamar Giles

Realistic Fiction YA

Delbert has had a crush on Kiera for most of his life. When she breaks up with her boyfriend, he seizes the opportunity and signs up for a volunteering gig with her, only to discover it's the Purity Pledge, a commitment to abstinence. He agrees to answer other members' questions about sex in exchange for them putting in a good word with Kiera. A hilarious book that explores teenage masculinity and sexuality.

The Rest of Us Just Live Here
by Patrick Ness

Fantasy YA

There are lots of stories about the "Chosen One," a person destined to be the hero of a story. But what about the people who go to school with them? Mikey is just trying to get through high school while everyone around him seems destined for something greater. A unique take on the hero's journey, full of sarcastic teen-friendly humor.

COMING OF AGE AND IDENTITY

Aristotle and Dante Discover the Secrets of the Universe
by Benjamin Alire Sáenz

Realistic Fiction YA

Set in late 1980s Texas, Aristotle Mendoza and Dante meet at a swimming pool where Aristotle goes to escape his family. Dante offers to teach him to swim and from there a friendship evolves into something new and surprising for both boys. A coming-of-age novel that beautifully explores friendship, queerness, and racial identity.

Darius the Great Is Not Okay by Adib Khorram

Realistic Fiction YA

Inspired by the author's own childhood experience, the story is about Darius, an Iranian American teenager struggling with depression, bullies, and fitting in. On his first trip to Iran, Darius discovers true friendship and wrestles with his identity. Full of humor and emotional power.

Empress of the World
by Sara Ryan

Realistic Fiction (YA) (S)

Nicola is spending the summer at the Siegel Institute, a program for gifted teens. As expected, she makes some new friends there. What she didn't expect was to fall in love . . . with a girl. A beautifully crafted love story with cool back matter that includes three graphic novel stories about the characters.

Frankly in Love by David Yoon

Realistic Fiction (YA) (AR)

Frank Li finds himself in a tight spot when he falls for a white girl, which breaks his parents' rule of only dating Koreans. A Korean friend is in a similar bind, so they pretend to date each other to satisfy their parents, while carrying on secret relationships with their not-Korean partners. Things don't turn out how Frank planned, however. This is a funny romance for readers who like John Green–type stories.

George by Alex Gino

Realistic Fiction (MG)

Melissa is transgender. Her family and classmates see her as a boy named George, but she knows that's not who she really is. When her teacher announces they'll be doing a production of *Charlotte's Web*, Melissa really wants the role of Charlotte. But since her teacher still sees her as George, she isn't allowed to try out. Undaunted, Melissa devises a plan to win the role and show everyone who she really is.

Marcelo in the Real World
by Francisco X. Stork

Realistic Fiction (YA) (AR)

Marcelo is a teen with Asperger's syndrome whose father wants him to gain "real world" experience by working at his law firm. Marcelo reluctantly agrees and ends up making some new friends on the job, and getting more "real world" experience than he ever bargained for. You'll be rooting for Marcelo all the way through this wonderful book.

Okay for Now by Gary D. Schmidt

Realistic Fiction

Son of an abusive father, fourteen-year-old Doug already has a trouble-maker reputation that's hard to shake. When he moves towns, he gets a chance to start over. With the help of new friend Lil, Doug finds refuge in the unlikeliest of places: the town library and the bird paintings of Audubon (the images decorate the novel). A wonderfully life-affirming story of friendship, redemption, and finding one's best self.

What Lane? by Torrey Maldonado

Realistic Fiction

Stephen is a twelve-year-old with a Black dad and a white mom. He moves between worlds, trying to figure out which "lane" is his. When he and his white friends decide to break into an abandoned warehouse, Stephen realizes he is seen and treated differently by some people in his community. This is a powerful yet accessible book to help start meaningful conversations about racism, white privilege, and racial profiling.

Other Words for Home by Jasmine Warga

Realistic Fiction

An incredibly beautiful book, written in verse, about Jude, a young girl who has to leave her Syrian home with only her mother to make a new life in the United States. This change comes with new and unfamiliar stressors as well as new excitement and opportunities. This is a story about losing your home and finding it again.

With the Fire on High by Elizabeth Acevedo

Realistic Fiction

After having a baby at the end of her freshman year of high school, Emoni must make some tough decisions as she navigates motherhood, school, and caring for her grandmother. She refuses to let obstacles stop her from pursuing her dream of becoming a chef. This is a beautiful book about a young woman determined to make her way.

SCI-FI AND FANTASY

The Art of Saving the World
by Corinne Duyvis

Sci-Fi (YA) (AR)

When Hazel was born, an interdimensional rift opened beside her house. Whenever she strays too far, the rift becomes unstable, forcing Hazel to stay close to home always. On her sixteenth birthday, things change when she comes face to face with *herself.* Another version of herself, anyway. A fascinating sci-fi book with a strong female protagonist.

Ash by Malinda Lo

Fantasy (YA)

In this reimagining of Cinderella, Ash is left with her evil stepmother after her father dies. Overwhelmed with grief, Ash retreats from the world until she meets Kaisa. Kaisa takes her out into the world, teaching her to hunt and rekindling Ash's ability to love. A romantic fairy tale that explores the transformative power of grief and love.

Children of Blood and Bone
by Tomi Adeyemi

Fantasy (YA) (AR) (S)

Zélie must hide her powers in Orïsha, a land where magic is banned. When her secret is revealed, she must flee the king's deadly soldiers. Forming an uneasy alliance with the king's son and daughter, Zélie must use her gifts to save her people and return magic to the land. An exciting fantasy rooted in African mythology.

The City of Ember
by Jeanne DuPrau

Sci-Fi (MG) (SA) (S)

Lina lives deep underground in the City of Ember. When she discovers clues left by the original builders, she searches for a passage out of her subterranean city and into the light of the world above. This gripping adventure is a good introduction to the dystopian genre for younger readers.

An Ember in the Ashes by Sabaa Tahir

Fantasy YA AR S

When Laia's brother is arrested by Martial forces, she seeks out the help of a resistance group. She infiltrates Blackcliff, a Martial training academy, and takes part in the Trials, a series of tests to decide who the next Emperor will be. A sensational fantasy series inspired by the author's Persian heritage.

Kiranmala and the Kingdom Beyond by Sayantani DasGupta

Fantasy MG S

Kiranmala goes from New Jersey sixth grader to Indian princess tasked with saving the world. Inspired by Bengali folktales, the author blends humor, American pop culture, sci-fi, and adventure with questions of Indian American identity and regular middle school angst. An excellent choice for kids who enjoy the Harry Potter or Rick Riordan series.

Legend by Marie Lu

Sci-Fi YA S

In the Republic, your future is determined by the Trials you take as a young child. June, one of the few to get a perfect score, is headed for a great career. Then her brother is murdered and she vows to catch the prime suspect, Day. Day failed the Trials and lives on the streets. As June chases Day, she learns more about her world and its many secrets. A thrilling dystopian series.

Scythe by Neal Shusterman

Sci-Fi YA AR S

In the future, death is a thing of the past. People no longer die of natural causes, but are "gleaned" by scythes. Scythes are humans tasked with controlling the overpopulation plaguing the world, deciding when and how people die. The two main characters are young would-be scythes learning the ropes. The author creates a unique and fascinating world that will bring up interesting ethical questions for discussion.

The True Meaning of Smekday by Adam Rex

Sci-Fi **MG** **RR** **S**

After Earth is invaded by aliens called the Boov, twelve-year-old Gratuity hits the road in the family station wagon, heading to Florida in search of her mother. On the way she meets a fugitive Boov who becomes an unlikely ally and friend. The story is funny and exciting, a perfect combo for younger kids. The audio version is also amazing—winner of Best Audiobook of the Year—and there's a movie version as well.

Wings of Fire series by Tui T. Sutherland

Fantasy **MG** **GN** **RR** **S**

This is a great series for anyone who enjoys fantasy, and especially dragons. With nineteen novels and four graphic novels currently, there is plenty of lore for readers to explore. There is also a graphic novel version of the series with gorgeous illustrations.

MYSTERIES AND THRILLERS

Elatsoe by Darcie Little Badger

Fantasy **YA** **RR**

A mystery/adventure/sci-fi novel that follows seventeen-year-old Elatsoe (a.k.a. Ellie) as she seeks justice for her murdered cousin. Ellie's Lipan Apache family has taught her to raise the ghosts of dead animals, and she uses her skills to embark on her first case as a paranormal investigator. The author blends the supernatural with realism to create an exciting and imaginative adventure grounded in Apache traditions and culture.

The Enola Holmes Mystery series by Nancy Springer

Historical Fiction **MG** **AR** **SA** **S**

This mystery follows Sherlock Holmes's kid sister, Enola, as she launches a career as a private detective. She must also outwit her older brothers, who want to put her in a boarding school to be trained as a "proper lady." Will appeal to adult Sherlock Holmes fans as well as younger fans of detective stories. The movie adaptation is also good fun.

Fake ID by Lamar Giles

Realistic Fiction

Nick and his family are in the Witness Protection Program due to mob ties. But when he meets Eli, editor of the school paper, Nick uncovers an intriguing but dangerous story. When Eli is found dead, Nick teams up with Eli's sister to find the murderer while trying to guard his secret past. A high-stakes thriller with a lot of action.

The Marrow Thieves by Cherie Dimaline

Sci-Fi YA AR

Set in a dystopian future where society is devasted by a mysterious plague: people have lost the ability to dream. Only Indigenous people can still dream, and they are hunted for their bone marrow in the hopes of developing a treatment. The author draws parallels to past genocide of Indigenous people in a very compelling sci-fi novel.

The Girl I Used to Be by April Henry

Realistic Fiction

Olivia's mother was killed when she was just three years old. Everyone suspected her father, but he disappeared. Years later, new evidence is uncovered proving her father was murdered the same day as her mother. Olivia is determined to find both her parents' killer . . . unless they find her first. A heart-pounding thriller by an expert mystery writer.

The Parker Inheritance by Varian Johnson

Realistic Fiction MG AR

After her grandmother dies, twelve-year-old Candace spends a summer in her home in Lambert, South Carolina, where she discovers a letter in the attic describing a treasure hidden in town. Candice searches for the riches with the boy next door, uncovering a long history of racism in Lambert. Set in the 1950s, the novel weaves the dark mysteries of the past into the children's present experience in the segregated south.

Skulduggery Pleasant by Derek Landy

Fantasy

When someone kills Stephanie's uncle and comes after her, she is thrust into a world of danger and magic. With the help of a skeleton named Skulduggery Pleasant, she must stop an evil sorcerer from finding a magic weapon, and solve the mystery of who murdered her uncle. An exciting story with plenty of action . . . and a talking skeleton!

The Third Twin by C. J. Omololu

Realistic Fiction

A thriller about identical twins Lexi and Ava who made up a third twin, Alicia, whom they blamed whenever they got into trouble. When they use Alicia as a cover to go out on dates, it all goes wrong when several of the guys turn up dead and the DNA suggests Alicia did it. Lexi must figure out if Alicia is real, or if Ava is the real killer.

We Were Liars by E. Lockhart

Realistic Fiction

Cadence spends her summers on Beechwood Island, which her rich family owns. When tragedy strikes the family, the reader must figure out who are "the liars" and what is true in this story full of twists and turns, mystery and murder, and a memorable ending.

York: The Shadow Cipher by Laura Ruby

Realistic Fiction

When they discover a mystery in the streets of New York, three middle schoolers must work together to solve a complex cipher in hopes it will lead them to treasure. But not everyone believes the cipher is real, and a real estate developer is threatening to demolish an essential part of the puzzle. If he succeeds, there may not be any cipher left to solve.

SOCIAL JUSTICE AND ACTIVISM

All American Boys by Jason Reynolds and Brendan Kiely

Realistic Fiction (YA)

After a police officer thinks Rashad stole a bag of chips and beats him so badly he ends up in the hospital, he is forced to contemplate what it means to be Black in America. Quinn, a white boy who looks up to the officer as a family friend, sees the injustice but is not sure how to act on it. They both go through individual journeys, Rashad in the hospital and Quinn in school, as they come to a greater understanding of racial issues in America. A powerful story with a strong message about social justice.

Amina's Voice by Hena Khan

Realistic Fiction (MG)

Amina is a young Pakistani American Muslim girl entering middle school and navigating the differences between home, school, and her Muslim community. One to avoid the spotlight, Amina comes into her own when her local mosque is vandalized and she uses her musical gift to comfort and unite her community.

Dear Martin by Nic Stone

Realistic Fiction (YA) (S)

Justyce is a Black teenager in a mostly white high school who finds common ground with new friend Manny. When they get into an altercation with a white cop who overhears them talking loudly in their car, things go wrong very quickly. Justyce is unfairly arrested but finds solace in the teachings of Martin Luther King Jr. A powerful book about racism, white supremacy, and the power of words.

Front Desk by Kelly Yang

Realistic Fiction (MG) (S)

Based on the author's own childhood, this story shows how ten-year-old Mia and her family navigate the challenges of coming to America. When the family finds work cleaning and running a motel, they secretly allow other immigrants to stay there for free behind the back of the cruel owner. This book tackles heavy subjects like poverty, racism, and bullying with humor and a light, hopeful tone.

Ghost Boys by Jewell Parker Rhodes

Realistic Fiction MG AR

When Jerome, a Black twelve-year-old, is shot and killed by police who mistake his toy gun for a real one, his ghost must come to terms with what happened. On this journey, he meets the ghost of Emmitt Till, who helps him understand how historical racism played a part in his death.

Monster by Walter Dean Myers

Realistic Fiction YA RR

When a drugstore owner is murdered, Steve Harmon is arrested and put on trial. Word on the street is that Steve was the lookout. To cope with the possibility of living the rest of his life in prison, Steve begins writing a movie script based on the events in his life. An award-winning story about surviving America's unjust criminal justice system.

The Only Road by Alexandra Diaz

Realistic Fiction MG

The story of two teen cousins who escape Guatemala and head to the United States after their family is terrorized by gang violence. Jaime and Ángela survive their perilous journey, eventually making their way to New Mexico. Based on true events, this story should inspire discussion about immigration, violence, and loss.

Speak by Laurie Halse Anderson

Realistic Fiction YA

This unforgettable novel is about high school freshman Melinda, who becomes an outcast after calling the police to come break up a party. In the aftermath, she stops speaking entirely. Through art, Melinda eventually faces what happened to her and finds the courage to speak out. This book deals with the difficult topics of rape and trauma.

We Didn't Ask for This by Adi Alsaid

Realistic Fiction YA AR

In a popular annual tradition, students at Central International School "lock" themselves in the building for one night each year. This year, however, a student decides to use the event to take a stand on climate change and *actually* locks all the students inside until demands are met. Told from multiple viewpoints, this novel explores activism among a privileged group of teenagers and the aftermath of the protest.

Zenobia July by Lisa Bunker

Realistic Fiction

The story of Zenobia July, a middle school hacker who moves from Arizona to Maine to live with her aunts. In Arizona she was a boy; now she's able to live openly as a girl. When someone posts hateful memes on her school's website, Zenobia uses her skills to catch the perpetrator. A touching story about identity and finding your true home.

HISTORICAL FICTION

Chains by Laurie Halse Anderson

Historical Fiction MG AR S

Set during the Revolutionary War, this is the story of thirteen-year-old Isabelle and her sister, Ruth, slaves who were promised freedom by their owner. When their owner dies, they become property of a cruel family of British loyalists. To help the

revolutionaries and gain her freedom, Isabelle spies on the family and passes on secret British plans.

Code Name Verity by Elizabeth Wein

Historical Fiction YA AR S

The story of two female British pilots and friends who crash their plane in enemy territory inside Nazi-occupied France in 1943. One pilot, Julie, is a spy who gets captured by the Nazis, sent to prison camp, and forced to write a detailed account of the British war effort. The other pilot, Maddie, attempts a daring rescue. Told in alternating voices along two different timelines, this is a thoroughly gripping spy novel.

Elijah of Buxton by Christopher Paul Curtis

Historical Fiction MG AR

Eleven-year-old Elijah lives in Buxton, Canada, in the 1850s. Buxton was founded by escaped American slaves and Elijah was the first child born free in the settlement. He never experienced the horrors of slavery, and when he journeys to the United States to stop a crime, he learns how valuable and fragile his freedom is. A superb, award-winning story about the Underground Railroad.

Esperanza Rising
by Pam Muñoz Ryan

Historical Fiction MG

After tragedy strikes, Esperanza must leave her comfortable, privileged life in Mexico and relocate with her mother to a California farm camp during the Great Depression. Esperanza has to adjust to a new culture, hard labor, and financial stress. When her mom gets sick, she joins the fight to improve working conditions and reunite her family.

How I Became a Ghost
by Tim Tingle

Historical Fiction YA RR S

The ghost of Isaac, a ten-year-old Chocktaw boy, narrates the story of his family fleeing their home in Mississippi and marching to the government-mandated reservation in Oklahoma, along the infamous Trail

of Tears. After Isaac is killed, he and a trio of other ghosts launch a bold rescue of a Chocktaw girl captured by soldiers.

The Night Diary
by Veera Hiranandani

Historical Fiction MG

Inspired by the real events of 1947 when India and Pakistan separated along religious lines, this novel takes the form of a diary. Twelve-year-old Nisha and her twin, Amil, must make a difficult journey with their widowed father from what is now Pakistan to India. The story explores the hardships of having a dual identity—part of Amil's family is Muslim, the other part Hindu—and finding a place where you belong.

One Crazy Summer
by Rita Williams-Garcia

Historical Fiction MG AR

Set in Oakland, California, 1968, where three sisters are visiting their mother for a summer. They spend some days at the People's Center, run by the Black Panthers, where they learn about the group's role in the Civil Rights movement. When their mother is arrested for her political activities, they have to fend for themselves until she is released from jail. A highly celebrated novel that will spark discussions about political activism.

Shooting Kabul by N. H. Senzai

Historical Fiction MG AR S

Set in San Francisco in the early 2000s, this novel tells the story of eleven-year-old Fadi, who flees Afghanistan with his family when the Taliban seized control. In the chaos of their escape, Fadi's younger sister is left behind. By entering a photography contest, Fadi seizes an opportunity to find his sister and reunite his family. Inspired by a similar family event, this story is a rich exploration of family, loss, and the refugee experience.

The War That Saved My Life by Kimberly Brubaker Bradley

Historical Fiction MG RR S

Set during World War II, Ada is hidden away in their apartment by her evil mother her entire life because of her twisted, unusable foot. As the bombs begin to fall and her little brother is sent out of London to the safety of the country, Ada makes a daring escape. She finds shelter in the home of curmudgeonly Susan. There Ada learns to read, ride a horse, and watch out for German spies. She also learns that she is much more than her disability. Ada's heart-wrenching journey will hook readers from page one.

We Are Not Free by Traci Chee

Historical Fiction YA AR

This novel follows the intertwining stories of fourteen Japanese American teens who are locked in internment camps after the bombing of Pearl Harbor. Each tale tells a different perspective as they navigate disappointment, anger, and a whole new world. The story is enriched with real photos and documents from this tragic time in US history.

SPORTS

Braced by Alyson Gerber

Realistic Fiction MG

Rachel is a middle schooler who learns she has scoliosis and will have to wear a brace day and night to correct the curvature of her spine. Inspired by the author's own experience, Rachel struggles with fears about losing her spot on the soccer team, being bullied about the brace, and whether it will ever get better. This inspiring story shows that what challenges us can also make us stronger than we ever imagined.

The Crossover
by Kwame Alexander

Free verse novel MG RR S

Told in free verse, this story follows twin brothers Josh and Jordan, who both love basketball but start drifting apart in their junior year of high school. A moving tale about growing up and the consequences that come with it.

Ghost by Jason Reynolds

Realistic Fiction MG RR S

After witnessing frightening scenes of domestic violence by his now-imprisoned father, Castle "Ghost" Crenshaw joins his middle school track team in hopes of turning his story around. Ghost and his teammates (whose stories are told in later books in the series) are all running toward the things they want for themselves and their lives.

Love Double Dutch!
by Doreen Spicer-Dannelly

Realistic Fiction MG RR

Thirteen-year-old MaKayla dreams of making it to the national Double Dutch jump roping championship at Madison Square Garden. Her dreams are foiled when her family moves to North Carolina and she has to make do with the available resources. The author also cowrote the screenplay for a 2007 movie about Double Dutch called *Jump In!*

Mexican WhiteBoy
by Matt de la Peña

Realistic Fiction YA RR

Danny is a seventeen-year-old student at a mostly white school where he does not fit in. And while he's a gifted baseball player, he always chokes when he plays at school. His mother is white and his father is Latinx, and when Danny spends the summer with his father's family, he struggles to make sense of his identity. Together with his new friend Uno, who is also biracial, Danny works on his game and the true meaning of belonging.

Peak by Roland Smith

Realistic Fiction   Ⓢ

Peak Marcello is a young climber arrested while scaling a building in New York City. A judge lets him go on the condition that he move to Thailand and live with his father. There he gets an opportunity to climb Mount Everest, which would make him the youngest person ever to summit. On the climb, he grapples with ethical dilemmas and life-or-death choices. A thrilling tale of a young climber growing up.

Takedown by Laura Shovan

Realistic Fiction ⓂⒼ

Lev isn't happy to have a girl as his wrestling partner, but Mickey won't let that stop her. Eventually, they become friends, but as they get closer to State finals, they realize only one of them can win. A fun story exploring girls joining male-dominated sports.

The Way Home Looks Now by Wendy Wan-Long Shang

Realistic Fiction ⓇⓇ

Twelve-year-old Peter joins a Little League team hoping to lift his mom's spirits after tragedy strikes their Chinese American family. Things don't go according to plan when Peter's father decides to coach the team, and even worse, his teammates dislike his dad's strict style. A great story about how a family's love of baseball can bring them together.

Whip It by Shauna Cross

Realistic Fiction ⓎⒶ ⓈⒶ

Bliss is a teen stuck in a tiny Texas town. She doesn't fit in. Her mom wants her to do pageants, but Bliss wants to join the roller derby instead. She joins a league, meets her people, and learns to smash, block, and jam on the track.

Zeroboxer by Fonda Lee

Sci-Fi

In this dystopian future, zero-gravity combat is Earth's most popular sport, and Carr Luka is its rising star. As Carr wins matches and becomes a celebrity with dreams of winning the championship, he discovers a criminal plot that will force him to make a devastating choice. A great book for kids who love sports stories and sci-fi.

NONFICTION

Brown Girl Dreaming
by Jacqueline Woodson

Verse memoir (MG) (RR)

A memoir in free verse tells of Woodson's childhood growing up as a Black girl during the civil rights movement. As a child, she often traveled between South Carolina and New York, and the poems contrast her experiences in both places. An excellent choice for discussions about racial justice and the unique power of poetry to convey emotion.

From an Idea to Nike: How Marketing Made Nike a Global Success by Lowey Bundy Sichol

Nonfiction (MG) (RR)

Whether your young reader is a sneakerhead or a budding entrepreneur, this book will inspire anyone interested in how an idea becomes a business. Filled with illustrations and infographics, the book starts with the early marketing campaigns of Nike and shows how the company's branding strategies evolved during its incredible growth.

Girls Who Rocked the World and Boys Who Rocked the World series by Michelle McCann

Biography (MG) (RR) (S)

The short, informative chapters in this unique series highlight the achievements of remarkable girls and boys who changed the world before the age of twenty. The girls span history, from Harriet Tubman to Ruth Bader Ginsburg, Malala, and Beyoncé. The boys range from historic heroes like George Washington Carver and Crazy Horse to modern icons like Bruce Lee and Bill Gates. The series shows kids that young people can have a profound impact on the world. Written by Michelle, one of our book club members.

Hidden Figures (Young Readers' Edition) by Margot Lee Shetterly

Nonfiction (MG) (AR) (SA)

This is an enjoyable adaptation for younger readers of the bestselling novel about four Black women who were critical to the success of the US space program. The story covers some pivotal movements in US history, including the civil rights movement, the fight for women's equality in the workplace, the Cold War, and the space race. A compelling, important read, and the movie is excellent too.

I Am Malala: How One Girl Stood Up for Education and Changed the World (Young Readers' Edition) by Malala Yousafzai, with Patricia McCormick

Memoir MG AR

In this true story, Malala's remote village in Pakistan was invaded by the Taliban, a fundamentalist military group that denied rights to girls and women. When girls were forbidden from going to school, fifteen-year-old Malala began speaking up for girls' education, and one day, while riding the bus, she was shot in the head by a Taliban gunman. She survived, and as she healed she continued to speak up for girls' rights. Her story and message spread around the world. The youngest winner of the Nobel Peace Prize, Malala is now a respected, international civil rights activist who has never stopped fighting for her beliefs.

Island Treasures: Growing Up in Cuba by Alma Flor Ada

Memoir MG AR

In this is a moving memoir about her childhood in Cuba, the author shares stories filled with the family and friends of her youth, as well as vivid descriptions of the foods, traditions, climate, and landscape of her homeland. A great book for discussing the history of Cuba, as well as your own family histories.

Jim Thorpe, the Original All-American by Joseph Bruchac

Biography MG RR

This unique, engaging first-person biographical novel tells the story of Jim Thorpe, one of the greatest, most versatile athletes of all time. A member of the Sac and Fox nation, Thorpe played not just one professional sport, he played three (baseball, basketball, and football). He also became the first Native American to win a gold medal in the Olympics—in 1912 he won two! His fascinating life, often omitted from the history books, is sure to make for an interesting discussion.

Laughing at My Nightmare by Shane Burcaw

Memoir (MG) (RR)

Twenty-one-year-old Shane Burcaw was born with spinal muscular atrophy, which has left him in a wheelchair and unable to do tasks many take for granted: walking, brushing his teeth, driving. Shane writes about his life—his struggles and triumphs—with incredible honesty and hilarious humor, from what it's like to have a girlfriend to how he goes to the bathroom. This uplifting, hysterical memoir is a joy to read, and gives readers an eye-opening perspective on what it's like to live with a life-threatening disability.

The Nazi Hunters: How a Team of Spies and Survivors Captured the World's Most Notorious Nazi by Neal Bascomb

Nonfiction (YA) (AR)

A historical narrative that tells of the search and capture of Adolf Eichmann, a Nazi war criminal who escaped prosecution by fleeing to Argentina. Readers follow along on the dramatic hunt for this criminal and are introduced to the horrors of the Holocaust as well as the courageous work done by the Nazi hunters who brought these criminals to justice.

Stamped: Racism, Antiracism, and You by Jason Reynolds and Ibram X. Kendi

Nonfiction (YA) (AR)

In the words of the authors: "This is not a history book. . . . This is a present book." In an engaging, fast-paced narrative, the authors explore America's history of white supremacy and challenge teens to look at the roots of racism and the institutions that uphold it. This book was intended to spark important conversation, and it certainly will.

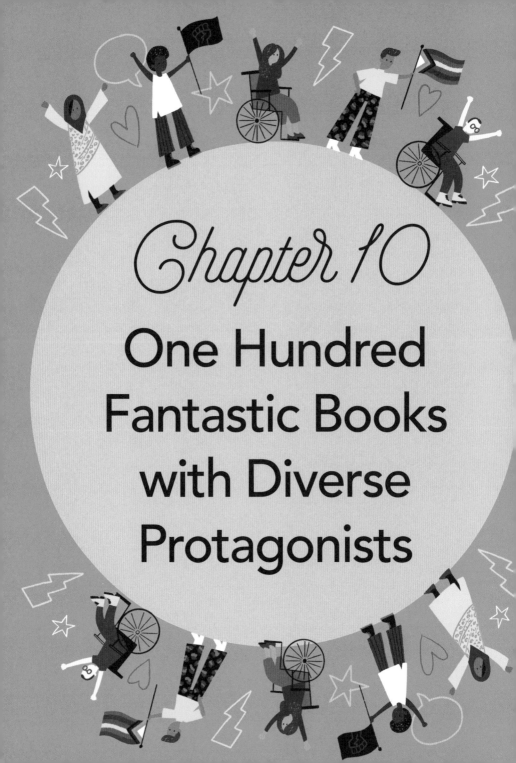

Chapter 10

One Hundred Fantastic Books with Diverse Protagonists

"What's the point of having a voice if you're gonna be silent in those moments you shouldn't be?"

—from *The Hate U Give*
by Angie Thomas

Our other lists are full of books with diverse protagonists and written by diverse authors. But we feel that to help begin to repair hundreds of years of white supremacy in children's literature, it is worth encouraging you and your group to read (and buy!) more books written by and about people who identify as BIPOC. The same goes for books written by and about girls and women, the LGBTQ+ community, and the disabled community. These groups have been underrepresented in literature for far too long. Reading books by diverse authors and about diverse characters should be part of your regular reading, not something special. This list gives you even more amazing writers and books to explore. And if you are wanting to find something for a particular reader or a particular discussion, this list is broken out by the identity of the protagonists. See Resources on page 198 for more places to look for diverse authors and books.

STRONG FEMALE PROTAGONISTS

Divergent by Veronica Roth
Sci-Fi YA

The Downstairs Girl by Stacey Lee
Historical Fiction YA

Escape from Aleppo by N. H. Senzai
Historical Fiction MG

Graceling by Kristin Cashore
Fantasy YA

The Invisible Life of Addie LaRue by V. E. Schwab
Fantasy YA

Mirage by Somaiya Daud
Fantasy YA

On the Come Up by Angie Thomas
Realistic Fiction YA

Saints and Misfits by S. K. Ali
Realistic Fiction YA

Watch Us Rise by Renée Watson
Realistic Fiction YA

A Wrinkle in Time by Madeleine L'Engle
Sci-Fi MG

Yaqui Delgado Wants to Kick Your Ass by Meg Medina
Realistic Fiction YA

BLACK PROTAGONISTS

American Street by Ibi Zoboi
Realistic Fiction YA

As Brave as You by Jason Reynolds
Realistic Fiction MG

Darius & Twig by Walter Dean Myers
Realistic Fiction YA

Dread Nation by Justina Ireland
Fantasy YA

The Great Greene Heist by Varian Johnson
Mystery MG

Opposite of Always by Justin A. Reynolds
Fantasy YA

This Side of Home by Renée Watson
Realistic Fiction YA

The Stars Beneath Our Feet by David Barclay Moore
Realistic Fiction MG

The Watsons Go to Birmingham—1963 by Christopher Paul Curtis
Historical Fiction MG

LATINX/AFRO-LATINX PROTAGONISTS

Blanca and Roja by Anna-Marie McLemore
Fantasy YA

Charlie Hernández and the League of Shadow by Ryan Calejo
Fantasy MG

Echo by Pam Muñoz Ryan
Fantasy MG

The First Rule of Punk by Celia C. Pérez
Realistic Fiction MG

Gabi, a Girl in Pieces by Isabel Quintero
Realistic Fiction YA

Letters from Cuba by Ruth Behar
Historical Fiction MG

Return to Sender by Julia Alvarez
Realistic Fiction MG

They Call Me Güero: A Border Kid's Poems by David Bowles
Realistic Fiction MG

We Set the Dark on Fire by Tehlor Kay Mejia
Fantasy YA

What Lane? by Torrey Maldonado
Realistic Fiction MG

EAST ASIAN/SOUTHEAST ASIAN PROTAGONISTS

Everything Asian by Sung J. Woo
Realistic Fiction MG

Hello Universe by Erin Entrada Kelly
Realistic Fiction MG

I'm OK by Patti Kim
Realistic Fiction MG

Jade City by Fonda Lee
Sci-Fi YA

Kira-Kira by Cynthia Kadohata
Realistic Fiction MG

Ninefox Gambit by Yoon Ha Lee
Fantasy YA

Not Your All-American Girl by Madelyn Rosenberg and Wendy Wan-Long Shang
Realistic Fiction MG

Spin the Dawn by Elizabeth Lim
Fantasy YA

To All the Boys I've Loved Before by Jenny Han
Realistic Fiction YA

Warcross by Marie Lu
Sci-Fi YA

SOUTH ASIAN/MIDDLE EASTERN PROTAGONISTS

Amal Unbound by Aisha Saeed
Realistic Fiction MG

Forward Me Back to You by Mitali Perkins
Realistic Fiction YA

A Girl Like That by Tanaz Bhathena
Realistic Fiction YA

Like a Love Story by Abdi Nazemian
Historical Fiction YA

The Long Ride by Marina Budhos
Historical Fiction MG

Love, Hate and Other Filters by Samira Ahmed
Realistic Fiction YA

Tell Me How You Really Feel by Aminah Mae Safi
Realistic Fiction YA

We Hunt the Flame by Hafsah Faizal
Fantasy YA

When Dimple Met Rishi by Sandhya Menon
Realistic Fiction YA

Whichwood by Tahereh Mafi
Fantasy MG

INDIGENOUS AMERICAN PROTAGONISTS

Black Elk's Vision: A Lakota Story by S. D. Nelson *Nonfiction* MG

The Clockwork Dynasty by Daniel H. Wilson
Sci-Fi YA

The Game of Silence by Louise Erdrich
Historical Fiction MG

Give Me Some Truth by Eric Gansworth
Realistic Fiction YA

Hearts Unbroken
by Cynthia Leitich Smith
Realistic Fiction YA

House of Purple Cedar
by Tim Tingle
Historical Fiction YA

I Can Make This Promise
by Christine Day
Realistic Fiction MG

Indian No More by Traci Sorell
Historical Fiction MG

The Marrow Thieves
by Cherie Dimaline
Mystery YA

Two Roads by Joseph Bruchac
Historical Fiction MG

LGBTQ+ PROTAGONISTS

Adaptation by Malinda Lo
Sci-Fi YA

Boy Meets Boy by David Levithan
Realistic Fiction YA

Felix Yz by Lisa Bunker
Sci-Fi MG

Girls of Paper and Fire
by Natasha Ngan
Fantasy YA

Hurricane Child
by Kacen Callender
Realistic Fiction MG

In the Role of Brie Hutchens
by Nicole Melleby
Realistic Fiction MG

*Middle School's a Drag, You
Better Werk!* by Greg Howard
Realistic Fiction MG

*The Miseducation of Cameron
Post* by Emily Danforth
Realistic Fiction YA

What if It's Us by Adam
Silvera and Becky Albertalli
Realistic Fiction YA

When the Moon Was Ours
by Anna-Marie McLemore
Fantasy YA

PROTAGONISTS WITH DISABILITIES

Challenger Deep by Neal
Shusterman, illustrated
by Brendan Shusterman
Realistic Fiction YA

El Deafo by Cece Bell
Realistic Fiction MG

Kinda Like Brothers by Coe Booth
Realistic Fiction MG

The Memory of Light
by Francisco X. Stork
Realistic Fiction YA

On the Edge of Gone
by Corinne Duyvis
Sci-Fi YA

Roll with It by Jamie Summer
Realistic Fiction MG

Temple Grandin: How the Girl Who Loved Cows Embraced Autism and Changed the World by Temple Grandin and Sy Montgomery
Nonfiction MG

Turtles All the Way Down
by John Green
Realistic Fiction YA

Two Girls Staring at the Ceiling by Lucy Frank
Realistic Fiction YA

The Weight of Our Sky
by Hanna Alkaf
Historical Fiction YA

BICULTURAL/ MULTICULTURAL PROTAGONISTS

Abby Spencer Goes to Bollywood by Varsha Bajaj
Realistic Fiction MG

The Agency series by Y. S. Lee
Historical Fiction YA

The Black Flamingo by Dean Atta
Realistic Fiction YA

Blended by Sharon Draper
Realistic Fiction MG

Brendan Buckley's Universe and Everything In It by Sundee T. Frazier
Realistic Fiction MG

Court of Fives Series by Kate Elliott
Fantasy YA

The Girl from Everywhere
by Heidi Heilig
Fantasy YA

Lupe Wong Won't Dance
by Donna Barba Higuera
Realistic Fiction MG

The Other Half of Happy
by Rebecca Balcárcel
Realistic Fiction MG

This Is Just a Test by Madelyn
Rosenberg and Wendy
Wan-Long Shang
Realistic Fiction MG

DIVERSE STORY COLLECTIONS

*All Out: The No-Longer
Secret Stories of Queer Teens
Throughout the Ages* edited
by Saundra Mitchell YA

*Ancestor Approved: Intertribal
Stories for Kids* edited
by Cynthia Leitich Smith MG

*Black Enough: Stories of Being
Young and Black in America*
edited by Ibi Zoboi YA

*Color Outside the Lines:
Stories About Love* edited
by Sangu Mandanna YA

*Come On In: 15 Stories About
Immigration and Finding Home*
edited by Adi Alsaid YA

*#NotYourPrincess: Voices of
Native American Women*
edited by Lisa Charleyboy and
Mary Beth Leatherdale YA

*Once Upon an Eid: Stories of Hope
and Joy by 15 Muslim Voices* edited
by S. K. Ali and Aisha Saeed MG

*Our Stories, Our Voices: 21 YA
Authors Get Real About Injustice,
Empowerment, and Growing
Up Female in America*
edited by Amy Reed YA

*Unbroken: 13 Stories Starring
Disabled Teens* edited by
Marieke Nijkamp YA

*We Rise, We Resist, We Raise
Our Voices* edited by Wade
and Cheryl Willis Hudson MG

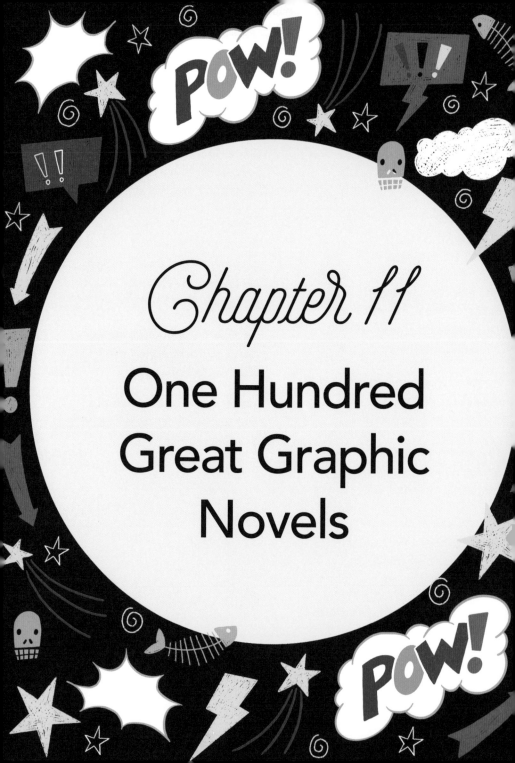

"I want you to always remember, no matter how bad things look to you, no matter how dark the night, when one door closes, don't worry, because another door opens."

—from *Bud, Not Buddy*
by Christopher Paul Curtis

There are excellent graphic novels for every age of reader, from picture books to young adult novels. Graphic novels have become one of the most popular sections at the library and a booming area of publishing. Because kids love them! Back in the old days, many teachers, librarians, and parents believed that comics and graphic novels weren't real books and didn't qualify as actual reading.

There is now plenty of research proving that is a bunch of hooey. Graphic novels are full of text that readers must decode and comprehend, plus plot and character development to follow. All this helps develop reading comprehension. Research shows that far from hindering a child's ability to read, graphic novels actually strengthen reading and other important skills. Reading graphic novels has the following benefits.

- *Kids may read above their reading level and dive into more challenging text.*

- *Less-proficient readers can jump into more complicated, meaty storylines. When they read more complex, compelling stories, they are motivated to continue reading.*

- *It builds comprehension and critical thinking skills.*

- *It teaches visual literacy and visual decoding—two very cool and helpful skills.*

- *It builds empathy by showing readers people who look different from them, and letting them step into their experience.*

- *It gets kids excited about reading!*

We are in a golden age of graphic novels right now. There are so many incredible artists and books to choose from. Where to begin? Here is a relatively short list of some great graphic novels for different ages and interests. You'll notice there are more graphic novels for middle grade readers, which reflects their popularity with that age group. But there are plenty of options for older readers as well, especially when you dive into graphic novel adaptations.

GRAPHIC NOVELS ARE MAGIC FOR RELUCTANT READERS:

Michelle

My daughter was a reluctant reader for years. I wasn't sure I would ever find the right book to hook her, but then a miracle happened! She found graphic novels. In graphic novels the text isn't long or intimidating and yet the stories are rich and engaging on a lot of different levels. My daughter ate them up! Every graphic novel we got she finished in a few hours, then would read again and again. This helped her build a reading habit and got her hungry for stories. Now, my sixteen-year-old is a voracious reader of all kinds of books. She still loves graphic novels the most and has read so many that she started her own website where she reviews them.

FRIENDSHIP AND ROMANCE

Amelia Rules! series by Jimmy Gownley
Realistic Fiction (MG)

Blankets by Craig Thompson
Realistic Fiction (YA)

Bloom by Kevin Panetta and Savanna Ganucheau
Realistic Fiction (YA)

Drama by Raina Telgemeier
Realistic Fiction (MG)

Emmie & Friends series by Terri Libenson
Realistic Fiction (MG)

Friends with Boys by Faith Erin Hicks
Realistic Fiction (YA)

Kiss Number 8 by Colleen AF Venable and Ellen T. Crenshaw
Realistic Fiction (YA)

Laura Dean Keeps Breaking Up With Me by Mariko Tamaki and Rosemary Valero-O'Connell
Realistic Fiction (YA)

Pumpkinheads by Rainbow Rowell and Faith Erin Hicks
Realistic Fiction (YA)

Real Friends by Shannon Hale and LeUyen Pham
Realistic Fiction (MG)

Secret Science Alliance by Eleanor Davis
Realistic Fiction (MG)

Slam! by Pamela Ribon and Veronica Fish
Realistic Fiction (YA)

Stargazing by Jen Wang
Realistic Fiction (MG)

This Was Our Pact by Ryan Andrews
Fantasy (YA)

COMING OF AGE AND IDENTITY

American Born Chinese by Gene Luen Yang
Realistic Fiction (YA)

Are You Listening? by Tillie Walden
Realistic Fiction (YA)

Be Prepared by Vera Brosgol
Realistic Fiction (MG)

Beautiful: A Girl's Trip through the Looking Glass by Marie D'Abreo
Realistic Fiction (YA)

El Deafo by Cece Bell
Realistic Fiction (MG)

Hey, Kiddo: How I Lost My Mother, Found My Father, and Dealt with Family Addiction by Jarrett J. Krosoczka
Realistic Fiction (YA)

In Real Life by Cory Doctorow and Jen Wang
Realistic Fiction (YA)

Jane, the Fox and Me by Fanny Britt and Isabelle Arsenault
Realistic Fiction (MG)

New Kid by Jerry Craft
Realistic Fiction (MG)

Roller Girl by Victoria Jamieson
Realistic Fiction (MG)

Smile by Raina Telgemeier
Realistic Fiction (MG)

Spinning by Tillie Walden
Realistic Fiction (YA)

Sunny series by Jennifer L. Holm and Matthew Holm
Realistic Fiction (MG)

This One Summer by Mariko Tamaki and Jillian Tamaki
Realistic Fiction (YA)

Tomboy by Liz Prince
Realistic Fiction YA

Twins by Varian Johnson
and Shannon Wright
Realistic Fiction MG

SCI-FI AND FANTASY

The Amulet series by Kazu Kibuishi
Sci-Fi MG

Anya's Ghost by Vera Brosgol
Fantasy MG

Cardboard by Doug TenNapel
Fantasy MG

Chronicles of Claudette
series by Jorge Aguirre
Fantasy MG

Cleopatra in Space series
by Mike Maihack
Sci-Fi MG

The Dam Keeper by Robert
Kondo and Dice Tsutsumi
Fantasy MG

Dragon Girl by Jeff Weigel
Fantasy MG

Fun Fun Fun World by
Yehudi Mercado
Sci-Fi MG

*Hereville: How Mirka Got Her
Sword* by Barry Deutsch
Fantasy MG

Ichiro by Ryan Inzana
Fantasy YA

Lowriders in Space by Cathy
Camper and Raul the Third
Fantasy MG

Lumberjanes by Grace Ellis,
Shannon Watters, and
various other artists
Fantasy MG

Mighty Jack series by Ben Hatke
Fantasy MG

Muddy Max by Elizabeth
Rusch and Mike Lawrence
Fantasy MG

Nightlights by Lorena Alvarez
Fantasy MG

Nimona by Noelle Stevenson
Fantasy YA

Pashmina by Nidhi Chanani
Fantasy (MG)

Princeless series by Jeremy Whitley and M. Goodwin
Fantasy (MG)

Rapunzel's Revenge by Shannon Hale and Dean Hale
Fantasy (MG)

Sci-Fu by Yehudi Mercado
Sci-Fi (MG)

Star Scouts by Mike Lawrence
Sci-Fi (MG)

Super Indian by Arigon Starr
Fantasy (MG)

Taproot by Keezy Young
Fantasy (YA)

The Time Museum by Matthew Loux
Fantasy (MG)

Trickster: Native American Tales, A Graphic Collection edited by Matt Dembicki
Fantasy (YA)

Zita the Spacegirl series by Ben Hatke
Sci-Fi (MG)

SOCIAL JUSTICE AND ACTIVISM

7 Generations: A Plains Cree Saga by David Robertson and Scott Henderson
Historical Fiction (MG)

Child Soldier by Jessica Dee Humphreys and Michel Chikwanine
Memoir (MG)

I Am Alfonso Jones by Tony Medina, John Jennings, and Stacey Robinson
Realistic Fiction (MG)

Illegal by Eoin Colfer, Andrew Donkin and Giovanni Rigano
Realistic Fiction (MG) (YA)

March trilogy by Congressman John Lewis, Andrew Aydin, and Nate Powell
Autobiography (YA)

Maus 1 and *2* by Art Spiegelman
Memoir (YA) (AD)

Persepolis by Marjane Satrapi
Memoir (YA) (AD)

The Silence of Our Friends by Mark Long, Jim Demonakos, and Nate Powell
Semi-Fictionalized Memoir YA

They Called Us Enemy by George Takei and Justin Eisinger
Memoir MG

War Brothers by Sharon E. McKay and Daniel Lafrance
Historical Fiction YA

HISTORICAL FICTION

Boxers and *Saints* by Gene Luen Yang
Historical Fiction YA

Delilah Dirk series by Tony Cliff
Historical Fiction MG

The Prince and the Dressmaker by Jen Wang
Historical Fiction YA

NONFICTION

The 14th Dalai Lama: A Manga Biography by Tetsu Saiwai
Biography MG

Almost American Girl: An Illustrated Memoir by Robin Ha
Memoir YA

Honor Girl: A Graphic Memoir by Maggie Thrash
Memoir YA

Little White Duck: A Childhood in China by Andrés Vera Martínez and Na Liu
Memoir MG

Nathan Hale's Hazardous Tales series by Nathan Hale
History MG

Primates: The Fearless Science of Jane Goodall, Dian Fossey, and Biruté Galdikas by Jim Ottaviani
Biography MG

Redbone: The True Story of a Native American Rock Band by Christian Staebler, Sonia Paoloni, and Thibault Balahy
History YA

Still I Rise: A Graphic History of African Americans by Roland Laird, Taneshia Laird, and Elihu "Adofo" Bey
History YA

Tales of the Mighty Code Talkers
by Lee Francis IV and others
History (MG)

When Stars Are Scattered
by Victoria Jamieson and
Omar Mohamed
Memoir (MG)

ADAPTATIONS

There are countless graphic novel adaptations of beloved middle grade, YA, and classic novels. You can look up just about any popular book, for any age, and there's a good chance you will find a graphic novel version of it. The publisher Graphic Classics does adaptations of most "classic novels" you can think of. Here is a smattering of adaptations to consider:

Anne Frank's Diary by Anne
Frank and David Polonsky
Memoir (MG)

Artemis Fowl by Eoin Colfer
and Stephen Gilpin
Fantasy (MG)

Coraline by Neil Gaiman
and P. Craig Russell
Fantasy (MG)

Dune by Brian Herbert, Kevin
J. Anderson, Raúl Allén,
and Patricia Martin
Fantasy (YA)

Frankenstein by Mary
Shelley and Gris Grimly
Fantasy (YA)

The Giver by Lois Lowry
and P. Craig Russell
Sci-Fi (MG)

The Golden Compass by Philip
Pullman and Clément Oubrerie
Fantasy (MG)

The Graveyard Book by Neil
Gaiman and P. Craig Russell
Fantasy (MG) (YA)

Jane by Charlotte Brontë,
Aline Brosh McKenna,
and Ramon K. Perez
Realistic Fiction (YA)

Kindred by Octavia Butler
and John Jennings
Historical Fiction (YA)

Legend by Marie Lu and Kaari
Sci-Fi (YA)

The Long Way Down by Jason Reynolds and Danica Novgorodoff
Realistic Fiction YA

Miss Peregrine's Home for Peculiar Children by Ransom Riggs and Cassandra Jean
Fantasy YA

Monster by Walter Dean Myers and Dawud Anyabwile
Realistic Fiction YA

The Mortal Instruments by Cassandra Clare and Cassandra Jean
Fantasy YA

Percy Jackson and the Olympians series by Rick Riordan and Robert Venditti
Fantasy MG

Speak by Laurie Halse Anderson and Emily Carroll
Realistic Fiction YA

To Kill a Mockingbird by Harper Lee and Fred Fordham
Realistic Fiction YA

Twilight by Stephenie Meyer and Young Kim
Fantasy YA

Uglies by Scott Westerfeld and Steven Cummings
Sci-Fi YA

A Wrinkle in Time by Madeleine L'Engle and Hope Larson
Sci-Fi MG

Resources

ONLINE BOOK REVIEWS AND LISTS

Each year more and more great books for kids come out. You can keep up with new releases, and read current reviews and recommendations on these websites:

Amazon

amazon.com

On each Amazon book page you will find a synopsis at the top, age range and genre information under Product Details, and awards and reviews under Editorial Reviews, including by reliable reviewers like *School Library Journal* and *Kirkus*.

Barnes & Noble

barnesandnoble.com

This bookseller website has a tab for Kids and another for Teens & YA. Under each you can search for books by reader age, subject, and author. They also provide a few specialized lists like "STEAM Books," "Kids' Classics," and "Graphic Novels for Young Readers."

Battle of the Books

battleofthebooks.org

A reading competition for kids in grades three through twelve that takes place in all fifty states. Librarians and teachers in each state pick the books for that state's readers, so there are some great regional authors on their lists. This is a great source for up-to-date and regional book recommendations for your book club.

Booklist

booklistreader.com

Created by the American Library Association (ALA), this website reviews new books for children and young adults. Older reviews are archived and searchable. You can also find links to the ALA's literary awards and recommended lists.

Common Sense Media

commonsensemedia.org

The Books tab at the top of the landing page lets you search for book reviews or recommended booklists. You can sort recommendations by age and genre. The reviews give you a book synopsis, areas of concern (violence, sex, drugs, etc.), reader reviews, plus a helpful section called "Talk to Your Kids About." It's a great place to look for potential discussion questions.

Indie Bound

indiebound.org

This website recommends great books in their Kids' Next List, chosen by employees at independent bookstores all over the country. The list is organized by age group.

Kate Messner

katemessner.com/authors-who-skype -with-classes-book-clubs-for-free/

Author Kate Messner has a great website with a huge list of children's book authors willing do book club visits for free.

Kirkus

kirkusreviews.com

One of the United States' oldest reviewers, *Kirkus* has been evaluating books for children and young adults since 1933. Their well-respected booklists are searchable by age and genre. Check their starred reviews, Best Books of the Year list, and Kirkus Prize winners.

NaNoWriMo

nanowrimo.org (for adults)

ywp.nanowrimo.org (for kids)

Each year, hundreds of thousands of writers participate in NaNoWriMo's challenge to write a full novel during the month of November. This organization doesn't provide book recommendations, but it's a great activity to do with any aspiring writers in your book club.

New York Times Book Review

nytimes.com/column/childrens-books

This website offers reviews and essays about children's and YA books.

Newbery Award

ala.org/alsc/awardsgrants/bookmedia/newbery

Established in 1922, this is one of the most prestigious awards for middle grade books and an excellent place to find options for kids ages eight to twelve.

Printz Award

ala.org/yalsa/printz-award

Established in 1999, this is the top US award for young adult books and an excellent place to find books for teens.

Publishers Weekly

publishersweekly.com

This online and print magazine is read by publishers, librarians, booksellers, and literary agents. It is one of the main places where people in the literary world go to find out about new books. This is an excellent resource for reviews and lists to explore when choosing books for your club.

School Library Journal

slj.com

This monthly magazine for school and public librarians is an excellent source for kids' book reviews and booklists. Check their starred reviews and Best Books of the Year list.

We Need Diverse Books

diversebooks.org

This group advocates for change in the publishing industry, to create more books by diverse writers and featuring diverse characters. Their website has excellent reviews and booklists, and their annual Walter Award (named for the late, great Walter Dean Myers) honors diverse books written by diverse authors.

YALSA

ala.org/yalsa/

The Young Adult Library Services Association, a division of the ALA, has a number of annual literary awards for teen books, plus great YA booklists, including "Amazing Audiobooks," "Great Graphic Novels," "Quick Picks for Reluctant YA Readers," and "Teens' Top Ten."

ONLINE RESOURCES FOR DIVERSE AUTHORS AND BOOKS

These sites have current reviews, awards, author interviews, and recommendations.

The American Indian Youth Literature Award

ailanet.org/activities/american-indian -youth-literature-award

Awards and reviews of children's books by American Indian authors and illustrators.

The Arab American Book Award

arabamericanmuseum.org/2019 -ba-winners

Awards and reviews of children's books by Arab American authors and illustrators.

The Asian/Pacific American Award for Literature

apalaweb.org/awards/literature-awards

Awards and reviews of children's books by Asian/Pacific American authors and illustrators.

Black Children's Books & Authors

bcbooksandauthors.com

Reviews and an online directory of Black children's lit authors and illustrators.

The Brown Bookshelf

thebrownbookshelf.com

Reviews and interviews showcasing children's books by Black creators.

Colours of Us

coloursofus.com

A directory of diverse books you can search by ethnicity and reader age.

The Coretta Scott King Book Award

ala.org/rt/emiert/cskbookawards

Honors outstanding Black authors.

Disability in Kidlit

disabilityinkidlit.com

Has reviews, interviews and recommendations by writers with disabilities.

The Lambda Literary Award

lambdaliterary.org

Champions LGBTQ+ books and authors.

Latinxs in Kid Lit

latinosinkidlit.com

Reviews and interviews with Latinx authors and illustrators.

The Middle East Book Awards

meoc.us/book-awards

Honors books that contribute to understanding the Middle East.

More Diverse

morediverse.com

Created by a Girl Scout in Tennessee; you can type in a book title and find a similar book with more diverse protagonists.

The Pura Belpré Award

ala.org/alsc/awardsgrants/bookmedia/belpre

Honors outstanding Latinx authors of kids' books.

The Schneider Family Book Award

ala.org/awardsgrants/schneider-family-book-award

For authors or books that honor disability experiences.

The South Asian Book Award

southasiabookaward.wisc.edu

Celebrates South Asian books and authors.

The Stonewall Book Award

ala.org/rt/rrt/award/stonewall

Honors LGBTQ+ books and authors.

The Walter Award

diversebooks.org/our-programs /walter-award

Celebrates diverse books written by diverse authors.

We Need Diverse Books

diversebooks.org

Has excellent reviews and lists of diverse books by diverse authors.

ONLINE USED BOOKSELLERS

Here are some great online resources for used books, which are cheaper than brand-new copies.

Better World Books

betterworldbooks.com

Better World Books donates a book to someone in need every time you purchase a used book. They collect and donate used books to literacy nonprofits around the world. They also offer e-delivery, where they will scan the book and send you a digital version in just a few hours. Shipping is free worldwide, and they pay for carbon offsets to minimize their ecological footprint.

Powell's Books

powells.com

This is the online version of Portland's beloved bookstore. Powell's has a wide range of new and used books, as well as great staff recommendations. Orders over $50 ship free.

Thrift Books

thriftbooks.com

Thrift Books partners with libraries and other vendors to make sure used books end up in good hands instead of the trash. They offer free shipping on US orders.

Acknowledgments

Making a book is a bit like having a child (but a whole lot cheaper). Our writing team would like to thank the many people who helped us bring this "baby" into the world, starting with the marvelous Amini sisters. Thank you, Ariana, for bringing us to Christina, and thank you, Christina, for helping us find the perfect publishing home.

A huge thanks to both our brilliant editors: Thank you, Deanne Katz, who made the excellent decision to publish our book and helped us get started with wise guidance, good humor, and cheerleading, all while caring for a brand-new baby (hey, it's never too early to start your book club, Deanne!). Thank you, Claire Gilhuly, who took the book from proposal to printer. You have been a wonderful collaborator, making this book so much better every step of the way!

Thank you to the entire Chronicle team who has helped transform our quirky idea into a beautiful book that will surely find its audience: Rachel Harrell, Magnolia Molcan, Cecilia Santini, Madeline Moe, Steve Kim, Cynthia Shannon, and Stephanie Seales. And one last thank-you to Liz Kay, whose incredible artwork made this book such a pleasure to look at.

We would also like to thank Michelle McCann for all her hard work motivating the rest of us to begin this project, write the book, and follow through with all the various stages. Without her guidance, expertise, and enthusiasm, this book would never have come to be.

Thank you to our friends who have been in the book club with us at various points over the years: Faith Simpson, Alex Cheriel, Jen and Ian Kevan, Kenan Smith, Alex Gutmann, Denise and Corinne Hare, Fiona and Sunny Karbowicz, Linda Raymond, and Elena Breedlove. Each of you added a unique spark to the group, which we were lucky to have.

Thank you to all the incredible teachers the kids have had over the years, at Winterhaven, where we started the book club, and then at various high schools. And the parents' teachers as well. Thank you, teachers, for helping inspire our shared love of reading!

Dominic and Ann thank their wonderful family members for talking with them about books, inserting Shakespeare quotes into daily conversation, and supporting them every step of the way: Mark, Catherine, and Oliver de Bettencourt (and their beloved dog, Maisy Fang de Bettencourt). They also thank the Multnomah County Library system and its amazing librarians for keeping them stocked with piles of books year after year.

Dana and Owen thank David for being an amazing husband and dad, and for holding down the fort while they were off at book club. Thank you to Finn; it's not always easy being the youngest, and yet you were always good natured about your brother getting to do all of the fun things first. Thank you for your understanding and humor. Dana also thanks Owen for joining her on this adventure: "I love that we enjoyed (and disliked) so many of the same books that we read together." Dana's final thanks goes to the good folks she taught with at Stanley Middle School. Her experience with book groups in her classroom sparked the idea for starting a book club with her own children. "Thanks to everyone at Stanley for the opportunities and support you gave me all those years ago."

Lissa thanks her younger son, Leo, for giving book club a try, and her husband, Matt, for appreciating her love of books and encouraging it in their sons. Noah thanks the other members of the book club for always putting up with his unusual book selections.

Kristin and Luci thank Ava, who gave book club a good try but ultimately decided she enjoys reading on her own terms, and Tom, who always supported the book club behind the scenes. They thank the rest of the Warden-Doherty extended family, who have inspired a love of reading in a wide variety of ways, always making books and reading topics of discussion. Last, Luci thanks their cats, Tulo and Cy, who always keep her lap warm when she reads.

Michelle thanks Fiona for having brilliant taste in graphic novels, giving the best recommendations, and helping choose the graphic novels for this book. She thanks Ronan for sharing this amazing literary adventure with her—it's been one of her favorite things they've done together. And her writing group, the Viva Scrivas, for telling her, "Hey, dummy, that's a great book idea!" Ronan thanks his mom for encouraging him to write this book in the first place and for editing all their writing. They both thank Jerry for being a great husband and father who reads more than anyone in the family and is always excited to talk books. And the rest of the extended McCann-VanRaden-Roehm-Trummer-Littlehales-Pendergrass clan, which is chock-full of hard-core book lovers who have shared and encouraged their passion for reading.

Finally, we want to thank the authors who wrote all the amazing books we read together. We got to go on hundreds of fascinating journeys, parents and kids together, thanks to you. The work you do is so important. Books bring joy and wonder, open hearts and minds, build understanding and compassion, and change lives. Thank you!